HEPTAPLUS

Six Days of Creation from *Biblia cum Concordantiis,*
Lyons, Jaques Sacon for Anton Koberger, 1515.

Pico della Mirandola

HEPTAPLUS

or

Discourse on the Seven Days of Creation

Translated
With an Introduction and Glossary by
Jessie Brewer McGaw

Philosophical Library
New York

Contents

ACKNOWLEDGMENTS

I owe many people a debt of gratitude for making this publication possible. The fact that no English translation had been made of the Latin philosophical treatise *Heptaplus* up to 1963 was brought to my attention by a member of my Methodist Church, Mr. Rolland Bradley, who was kind enough to lend me his copy of the 1942 Garin Edition, which I used throughout. Various friends and staff members at the University of Houston have encouraged and assisted me in numerous ways. In the early part of 1964, I was awarded a sixteen-hundred-dollar grant from the University of Houston through the continued efforts of Dr. Patrick J. Nicholson, Vice-President in charge of University Development. I was aided more than I can say by the former M.D. Anderson Professor of Philosophy and Religion at the University of Houston, the late Winfred E. Garrison, who advised me about the philosophical thought and interpretation. I also owe a debt of gratitude to the late Dr. Lionel Stevenson, visiting professor from Duke University, for his careful reading of the manuscript and helpful suggestions and advice. Without the encouragement and guidance of the English Department Chairman, Dr. William B. Hunter, Jr. and the support of Dr. John C. Guilds, Dean of Humanities and Fine Arts, I might have given up on this ambitious endeavor many times. My thanks are due in full measure to the University of Houston Publications Committee, chaired by Dr. Steven C. Welch, and also to the University of Houston Research Committee's Subcommittee on Limited Grants-in-Aid, chaired by Dr. Francis B. Smith, for support in the publication. I am indebted to Dr. Patrick G. Hogan, Jr.

for suggesting the inclusion of the glossary. Special thanks go to my typists Mrs. Pat de Hoop, Mrs. Christine Morris, Ms. Kay Copeland, and Ms. Lynda Kaye, whose patience in deciphering my various corrected copies and whose nimble fingers made this all readable. My appreciation is also due to those who have faced the rigors of this subject and whose books I have mentioned in my bibliography and footnotes. Special thanks are also owed to Mrs. Rose Morse, Associate Director of the Philosophical Library, for her unfailing and prompt cooperation. Among the many others who expressed interest and encouragement are Mrs. Gene H. Jackson, Dr. John M. Meador, Dr. Helen Moore Eaker, Dr. Roberta Weldon, Dr. William Lee Pryor, Mr. Richard G. Barnes, Mrs. Ray L. Dudley, Mrs. G. S. Holm, and Mrs. Lyndall Finley Wortham. For their patience, advice, and tolerance, I owe a special note of gratitude to my sister and her husband, Dr. and Mrs. Joseph M. Doggett, and my children, Miriam McGaw Dennis and Vernon Howard McGaw.

                                                                    J. B. M.

Houston, Texas
May, 1976

HEPTAPLUS

INTRODUCTION

The Historical Setting: Renaissance Humanism.

Like the entire movement of the Renaissance, Humanism had its source in Italy, a country which had maintained its ancient greatness and become the cradle of the Roman Catholic Church. Humanism has been variously defined. In the 15th century it represented, on one hand, a break with a superstitious attitude and an authoritarian intellectual method, and, on the other hand, a turning back to Greek and Latin writers as a source of inspiration and guidance. This era was characterized by a new attitude in which the center of reference became man rather than God.

Humanism actually represented a state of mind rather than a movement between two chronological periods. Moreover, this spirit of Humanism was manifest even earlier through such thinkers as Albertus Magnus, Roger Bacon, Thomas Aquinas, St. Francis, Boccaccio, and Petrarch. This radical change in the intellectual outlook in Europe was prompted by the immigration of Byzantine refugee-scholars after the fall to the Turks of Constantinople, the Eastern Capitol of the Roman Empire. With these new-comers came a rediscovery of the lost manuscripts of many forgotten classics of Latin and Greek literature, which became much treasured by the learned. A renewed interest in the ancient classics was further encouraged by Renaissance Pope Nicholas V, who founded the Vatican Library.

Thus, it came about that in this classical revival, the ancient Greek and Roman tradition became absorbed by the Christian tradition. The value of the renewed interest in the Classics was well stated by

Matthew Arnold. To paraphrase him, the equal combination of Hebraism with its strict obedience to conscience and of Hellenism with its spontaneity of consciousness would lead to that perfect balance which is the aim of culture. To the Humanists, the most exciting aspect of these classical writings was that they espoused a philosophy for living in this world, rather than a concern for life after death.

It may be remembered that the Roman Cicero, a transmitter of Greek thought, had been a great influence on Augustine. In Book III of his *Confessions*, Augustine lamented that he had cared more for the study of Latin in his youth than reading the Scriptures; however, he was so deeply moved by reading Cicero's "Hortensius," an exhortation to the study of philosophy, that this proved to be an instrument in St. Augustine's conversion to Christianity.

This acceptance of pagan literature by the Christian world was naturally not achieved without a struggle. While many of the fathers of the Church treasured the classics, it is true that they never attacked classical literature more often than during the Renaissance. Medieval men were far from unfamiliar with classical thought; it was a part of their background. Just as captive Greece, becoming a part of the Roman Empire, gave to its captor Rome its culture and ideas on religion, government, art, architecture, and literature; so in time, as the former dominance of Rome fell to that of the Medieval Church, the Church became the recipient of the Greco-Roman culture. In a sense, the Italian Humanists were direct heirs of the ancient Romans, who had been creative borrowers of the Greeks. In certain ways the Renaissance seemed retrogressive in that there was some rejection of the vernacular Latin of the Medieval Ages in favor of Ciceronian prose.

From the second half of the fifteenth century on, the influence of Humanism on literary consciousness and good literary style plus the spread of printing plants by Aldus Manutius and others vastly encouraged literary effort. Erasmus, the model for the enlightened Humanist, spent much of his life and energy in producing a new Latin testament and in translating many of the Greek classics. Aided by the extensive correspondence of Erasmus, Humanists throughout Europe were able to keep in touch with one another.

As the assimilation of Greek and Roman literature became more and more complete, it became increasingly noted that this assimilation dominated the creative work of the aritsts. Humanists displayed their ability by writing poems and plays which might be represented as newly discovered texts of ancient authors. It was said that one of Michelangelo's first pieces of sculpture was a statue later to be sold as a recovered Greek marble. Architecture provided a good example of the connection between art and philosophy through Alberti's experimentation with symmetrical circular churches. Behind this innovation in architectural forms lay the increasing popularity of Platonic and Neo-Platonic ideas, with their emphasis on the perfection of the circle and the possibility of expressing all relationships in terms of mathematical harmonies. Although the art and literature at this time were repetitions of the art and literature from the ancient world, architecture created new forms based on classical philosophy.

Much of the art of Medieval Christianity had dealt with suffering and death. Following the Renaissance, however, art turned from expressing sufferings to expressing the joy of living. The Renaissance attempted to Christianize ancient pagan art by using it for the embellishment of cathedrals and palaces. The people, on the whole, continued to find pleasure in display and parade, in worship at the shrine of a miracle, or in a dogma they hardly grasped.

Moreover, the people had not rejected traditional transcendentalism. Even among the avowed Humanists, many had no thought of consciously renouncing the Christian religion and the Church. Movements for reform of the Church and society at the end of the fifteenth century were inspired by the new scholarship and the new philosophy because there was a common belief in the power of the human intellect to bring about institutional and moral improvement. Many reforms emphasized nature rather than grace, ethics rather than theology, and action rather than contemplation.

The Italian Renaissance, with its attendant Humanism, was a complex occurrence in the evolution of human thought. After a long influence by Judeo-Christianity, this confrontation of Classical and Christian ideologies produced a period of intensive philosophical inquiry.

3

The Florentine Platonist: Pico della Mirandola, 1463-1494.

It was into this scene of merging cultures that there appeared Pico della Mirandola, who served as an excellent example of how the confrontation of classical and Christian ideologies affected one of the great thinkers of this period. Along with such fifteenth century Renaissance thinkers as Erasmus, Leonardo da Vinci, Machiavelli, Michelangelo, and Copernicus, Pico had opportunities to study many concepts on a very wide range of subjects. A mastery of many subjects, during the brief thirty-one year span of his life, made Pico the amazing person he was.

Giovanni Pico was born in Mirandola in 1463. He was the younger son in the family of the counts of Mirandola and Concordia, who ruled as feudal lords over a small territory in northern Italy and claimed descent from the Roman Emperor Constantine. Pico, who was considered a child prodigy, received a humanistic education at home. Being encouraged by his mother for a career in the Church, he was named papal protonotary at the age of ten and began to study cannon law at Bologna in 1477.

Tiring of the life at the university after two years, he spent the next several years among various schools in Italy and France, where he acquired Greek and Latin learning and philosophy. After studying at the University of Ferrara, he attended the University of Padua as a pupil of the Jewish Alverroist Elia del Medigo and the Aristotelian Ermolao Barbaro. During this time, he was in touch with Humanist scholars in various places and collected a valuable personal library on Greek, Roman, Hebrew, Chaldean, and Arabic philosophy. A turning point in his life was his close association with the Platonic Academy in Florence, where he was strongly influenced by the Platonists Ficino and Politian. There he entered the circle of Lorenzo the Magnificent of the prominent Medici family, and, from time to time, he was to return to this group. He studied for a while at the University of Paris, the chief center of Scholastic philosophy and theology. Later in Perugia, he studied Hebrew and Arabic under the guidance of several Jewish teachers of the Cabala.

Endowed with this remarkable background and possessed with a confidence that was inspired by an atmosphere of critical evaluation, Pico formulated his first major work. By the end of 1486, he had composed his famous nine hundred theses and offered to defend them publicly with some of the most eminent scholars of Europe. These *Conclusions*, as he called them, covered almost every aspect of learning: forty-five were extracted from the works of St. Thomas, seventeen from Albertus Magnus, and twenty-two from Duns Scotus. A commission, appointed by Pope Innocent VIII to study the theses, declared thirteen of the theses heretical, prohibited the debate, and excommunicated Pico. When Pico published a defense of these thirteen theses, the Pope condemned all nine hundred.

Pico then fled to France and was held in prison at the request of a papal envoy until several Italian princes established parole permitting him to live in Florence, where he settled under the personal protection of Lorenzo de' Medici. In 1489, he again published a work, *Heptaplus*, which was declared heretical. At this point, Pico seemed to renounce his Humanistic beliefs as he became the docile pupil of Savonarola, a radical reform priest who had followed him from the time he was a student at Ferrara. Savonarola preached an eternal burning Hell for those who drifted away from the Church to follow Humanistic beliefs. The preachings of Savonarola were regarded as being responsible for the downfall of the Medici family and the destruction of many priceless manuscripts and valuable works of art. Savonarola was finally declared a heretic by the Pope and burned at the stake.

A little known fact about Pico's life was his marriage in 1491 to a Carofa heiress, whose dowry enabled him to purchase the hereditary title to the principate of Mirandola from his uncle, Giovanni Pico. This uncle had been responsible for Pico's start in his literary and philosophical endeavors.

In the years immediately after his marriage, Pico entered into correspondence with several men of political and intellectual prominence. During this period, he wrote *De Ente Et Uno*, an effort to reconcile the controversy between the Platonists and the Aristotelians, and *Oratio De Hominis Dignitate*, which is considered to be the manifesto of the Renaissance and of Humanism. These writings were not published until 1496, when Pico's nephew, Giovan Francesco, included them in a posthumous edition. Under the influence of Savonarola, the same nephew wrote a biography of Pico. This has been the source of the tradition concerning Pico's wild youth, sudden conversion, and ascetic later years. Many distortions of Pico's ideas were made in these memoirs.

Pico was reconverted to Christianity and humbly submitted to the Church his "Apologia," in which he was able to explain the condemned theses to the satisfaction of the Church. His early death from a fever cut short his masterpiece, the *Symphonia Platonis et Aristotelis*, and may have prevented more serious embroilment with the Church at Rome.

Pico died at the end of 1494, shortly after Pope Alexander VI lifted the ban on his theses. Hence at an early age, his life of promise was cut short before he had developed his ideas into a mature system of thought. He was, nevertheless, very influential on the enlightened religious attitudes of Humanists everywhere. Sir Thomas More was a great admirer of the Florentine Platonist, whose biography he wrote. With both classicist and Christian beliefs, with both Humanistic and Scholastic beliefs, Pico's breadth of knowledge and universal concept distinguished him from all the other thinkers of his time.

Heptaplus.

Perhaps inspired by one of his feudal titles, Count Concordia, Pico wrote the *Heptaplus* in an effort to reconcile the account which pagan philosophy gave of the creation of the world with the account given in the books of Moses: the *Timaeus* of Plato with *Genesis*, for instance.

The Hebrew and Christian religious tradition had its basis in Scripture and faith, whereas Platonic philosophy had its basis in reason and in the authority of ancient philosophers. Plato had been the main stimulus to Renaissance philosophy, especially after Ficino's translation of his works into Latin. The Neoplatonist Plotinus, with his mystical and speculative aspects, seemed to have had an especial appeal to Pico. However, as the Glossary indicates, Pico did not stop with the Greek philosophers in this synthesis. Because of his historical view of philosophy and religion, his curiosity encompassed much more ancient philosophy, including Arabic thought, the Hermetic writings, the Chaldaic Oracles, the Orphic hymns, and the golden symbols of Pythagoras. Furthermore, as the first Western scholar who became closely acquainted with the Jewish Cabala, Pico tried to

6

reconcile the Cabala also with Christian theology and to associate it with the Platonist tradition.

At the beginning of the book, a dedicatory greeting from Roberto Salviati, the publisher of the 1489 original edition, was made to Lorenzo de' Medici. This preface to *Heptaplus* had praise for both Medici and Pico. In the Proem, Pico also dedicated *Heptaplus* to Lorenzo because of his admiration for him and his appreciation for being permitted to live under his protection. Following the Pope's condemnation, Pico lived in Lorenzo's villa at Fiesole, where he composed the *Heptaplus*.

In Pico's explanation for the difficulty in interpreting *Genesis*, he referred to the intentional allegorical obscurity so that an interpretation might not be possible for the unprepared. He mentioned, also, the provision of the Mosaic law whereby doctrines were not fully revealed, as in a parable, but left to be gleaned by the more needy. The policy of the ancient world was concealment of its mysteries.

Using Medieval cosmology, Pico divided the created world into three groupings: the intelligences or angels, the heavenly or celestial bodies, and the corruptible earthly bodies. Pico related how this hierarchy was suggested in *Genesis*, and how Moses symbolically pointed out the facts of natural science as Pico recognized them. Believing that Biblical concepts represented philosophical concepts, Pico thought Moses had foreseen the findings of the philosophers about form and matter. He stated that these three parts of the world were fashioned clearly by Moses in the construction of his tabernacle into three parts. To illustrate that the three parts of the world have similar qualities, he used heat as an example:

Among us, heat is an elemental quality; in the celestial world, it is a calorific power [virtue]; in the angelic minds, it is an idea of warmth. I shall speak more clearly: among us, fire is a physical element; the sun is fire in the sky, the celestial world; and in the region above man, fire is the seraphic intellect. But see how they differ: the elemental fire burns, the celestial fire enlivens, and the supercelestial fire loves.

Pico's description of the planets and divisions in the Celestial World was somewhat similar to Dante's concept of Paradise, with

7

which he was familiar. Pico's *Adversus Astrologos* had been an ambitious attempt to criticize the errors of the astrologers. He was opposed to the teachings of the astrologers because the doctrine would subject man to forces above him and prevent him from being a free moral agent.

Tending toward a natural religion, Pico believed in the necessity of creation, in the "Great Chain of Being," and in a Supreme Maker, who made man in his own image. He regarded the Platonic idea of man as an intermediary between the physical and spiritual worlds to be comparable to the Biblical notion of man being an image of God.

Pico greatly enhanced his account by analogies, double meanings of words, and ritualistic symbols. In the fourth chapter of the Seventh Exposition, following the vogue of his age, he devoted himself at great length to Biblical prophecy. As a climax to this, in an epilogue, he concluded with his examination of the first phrase in the Hebrew Genesis: "In the beginning." He virtually played a game of anagrams by arranging letters selected from the Hebrew letters in that phrase.

Thought-provoking, and even fantastic, were some of Pico's interpretations. He approached the problem of harmonizing the Christian and Hebrew traditions with a more philosophical spirit than most of his predecessors. He was not concerned with merely reconciling the hostile systems of thought or with emphasizing the errors of the Jews and the Gentiles. Instead, Pico believed that "behind apparent diversity lay unity." In retrospect, the universal conception of this man must have sown some seeds of current theological ecumenism. As Pico concluded in *Heptaplus*,

> Just as the whole world is one in the totality of its parts, so also like this, at the end, it is one with its Maker. Let us also imitate the holy agreement of the world, so that we may be one together in mutual love, and that simultaneously, through the true love of God, we may all happily ascend as one with Him.

Notes on Translation.

Mindful of the Italian proverb, "Traduttore, Traditore," or "Translator, Traitor," I have endeavored to make my translation as literal as it could be in keeping with the subject.

On the whole, Pico wrote in good Classical Latin with touches of Medieval Latin. Usually there was proper balance in his sentences despite their inordinate length, occasionally running from ten to fifteen lines. Following his word order rather closely, I was prone to keep his original sentence structure, unless I considered the meaning to be improved by changing it. Because of rare paragraph breaks, I arbitrarily made them myself and frequently followed the indications made in the Italian translation that was also in the 1942 Garin edition that I used [see bibliography].

I have tried to avoid giving *Heptaplus* new sense through words that are current today by trying to keep my vocabulary within the context of the King James Version of the Bible. Wishing to use this time-hallowed vocabulary, I read passages in it or the Latin *Vulgate* relating to the text in order to familiarize myself with the words used. This was especially helpful in translating religious terms not found in my dictionaries or when familiar words did not seem to fit properly into the context where they were used. For example, "study to keep quiet" is an example of the archaic meaning of "study" that denotes putting forth great effort. It became apparent that "thou," "thy," "mine," "thee," and the reflexive-intensive "thyself" refer to one person, while the forms "ye," "your," "yours," "you," and "yourself" always refer to more than one. Obviously, "Abraham's chest" becomes "the bosom of Abraham," and "the favorite sons" become "the chosen people." Phrases like "the hiding place" and "the promised land" were easy to recognize. However, Pico's use of the Latin word "virtus," usually meaning "manliness," "virtue," or "courage" needed to be translated as "power." Why didn't he use "vis"? Many questions go unanswered.

I have consciously taken very few liberties with the text. When a personal touch seemed to be indicated, I have changed Pico's editorial "we" to the singular form "I." A few tense changes have been made for consistency, and all nouns and pronouns pertaining to the Deity have been capitalized. I have tried to avoid capturing certain aspects of his work at the cost of sacrificing others.

As often as possible I used the English derivative for the Latin word, and I noticed that the King James Version contained a multitude of Latin derivatives: multitude, creation, providence, damnation, salvation, testament, scriptures, redemption, adoption, reconciliation, justification, regeneration, perseverence, elation, consummation, predestination, conversion, inspiration, revelation, and on and on. Why substitute some common, homely words of Anglo-Saxon origin for those majestic, resounding, mouth-filling Latin words? "O Tempora! O Mores," Cicero would exclaim at Latin's present disrepute.

I have attempted to retain some of the literary qualities of Pico, such as his dignity, precision, and freedom of expression. Otherwise, I might have been guilty of writing "translation Latin," which makes a reliable "pony," as any student of a foreign language knows, even though it does a disservice to the literature. With the able assistance of the former M.D. Anderson, Professor of Philosophy and Religion at the University of Houston, Winfred E. Garrison, who recommended on many occasions the most exact word according to the philosophical context and sequence of thought, I have aimed at retaining Pico's style as well as meaning.

I am including a Glossary to define proper names, especially those of ancient origin. Most of my footnote references were obligingly given in the Garin edition, and the Biblical references come from the King James Bible.

Translations can never be wholly accurate, and they do vary among themselves because they filter one person's thoughts through another person's words. With each translation being an echo of the original, there is need for several versions so that there will be a more complete understanding, not only of the author's ideas expressed but also of his tone and attitude toward life. Pico is a vastly interesting author to know.

ROBERTO SALVIATI GREETS LORENZO DEI MEDICI[1]

Because I am endowed by character, o very distinguished Lorenzo, and so ordained by nature to feel that nothing is better than to love, to cherish and to respect those who are either superior in character or remarkable in training, I could not but love and admire above everyone else your friend Pico della Mirandola, a man most truly deserving of the highest respect. And because he recently dedicated to you a book about the seven-fold account of the six days of *Genesis*, which is the first fruits of his studies, a work most excellent not only in my judgment but in the judgment of all, I wanted to take pains that this book might be published in a faultless edition at my expense, doubting not at all that I, by doing so, would satisfy, at the same time, both my love for him and the general need of scholars. Added to that was the fact that I also hoped to do something not unpleasing to you if those natural and divine mysteries which he communicated to you should finally be made common to all. Farewell.

HEPTAPLUS OF GIOVANNI

PICO DELLA MIRANDOLA

HEPTAPLUS OF GIOVANNI PICO DELLA MIRANDOLA

The Seven-fold Narration of the Six Days of *Genesis* to Lorenzo dei Medici.

PROEM

Lorenzo dei Medici, emulation of your studies moved me to review the secret books of Moses; since last winter I observed that in whatever leisure was allowed by the republic you enjoyed no other work more often and with more pleasure than in that reading.

Also a personal reason motivated me: since in the other one of my works now growing long under your patronage and in your name, in which I tried not only to free from any false idea and subterfuge but also to clarify with the torches of my interpretation the hymns of David, translated by ''the Seventy''[1] and still resounding in the church, no discussion at all has been found more useful and fruitful than that of those books (as I truly said), nothing now can be found more suited and, better yet, more useful. Actually, in these days it happened I was concerned with the making of the world and those famous works of the six days in which we have a good reason to believe all the secrets of nature are contained.

For I pass over the fact that our Prophet received all this by the inspiration of God and the dictation of the heavenly Spirit, Master of all truths. Has not the testimony, not only of our people but of His own

15

people, and of the Gentiles, shown this same one to us as absolutely the most learned in human knowledge and in all science and literature? There exists among the Hebrews, under the name of the most sapient Solomon, a book entitled *The Wisdom*, which is not the work of Philo that we have now, but another one written in that esoteric language called "Hierosolyma," in which the author as an interpretor of the nature of things, it is thought, confesses that he received all his wisdom of this kind from the depths of Mosaic Law.

So far as we are concerned, both Luke and Philo, moreover, are very authoritative testimonies that Moses was very learned in all Egyptian doctrines.[2] And all the Greeks who have been considered superior—Pythagoras, Plato, Empedocles, Democritus—used the Egyptians as masters. It is a well-known saying of the philosopher Numenius[3] that Plato was nothing else but an Attic Moses. Also the Pythagorean Hermippus attests that Pythagoras transferred many things from the Mosaic Law into his own philosophy.[4] Accordingly, if in his books Moses appears naive and sometimes more an inexperienced popularizer than a philosopher, or theologian, or creator of great wisdom; nevertheless, let us keep in mind that it was a famous custom of ancient seers simply not to write of divine matters or to write of them dissemblingly; hence, they are called mysteries (things that are not hidden are not mysteries); this has been observed by the Indians, by the Ethiopians, to whom the surname was given because of their nakedness, and by the Egyptians; also the Sphinxes in front of the temples insinuated this. Taught by them, Pythagoras became a master of silence; and he himself did not commit anything to writing, except only a very few things which he gave in custody to his daughter Dama. In fact, those golden poems that are circulated are not of Pythagoras, as commonly believed even by the most educated, but of Philolaus.[5] The Phythagoreans with continuous tradition have guarded the custom very religiously. Lysis deplores that it was violated by Hipparchus. Finally, Porphyry is the authority by which the disciples of Ammonius—Origin, Plotinus, and Herennius—swore.[6]

Thus, our Plato hid his beliefs with masks of allegory, a veil of myths, mathematical images, and obscure disclosures of late events so that he himself declared in his *Epistles*[7] that from what he wrote no one would clearly understand his ideas on divine things, and likewise he has proven this to the incredulous.

Therefore, if we consider Moses' writings commonplace just because at first sight they are rough and unpolished, for the same reason let us condemn for roughness and want of knowledge all the ancient philosophers whom we venerate as masters of all wisdom. We discern the same thing adhered to in the church: Jesus Christ, the image of the substance of God, preached the Gospel rather than wrote it. In fact, He preached to the masses in parables, and separately, to the few disciples to whom it was given to understand the mysteries of the kingdom of heaven plainly without figures of speech. Nor did Jesus reveal everything to those few, because they were not ready for everything, and they could not bear the burden of many things until the coming of the Holy Ghost taught them all truth. If the few disciples of the Lord, chosen from so many thousands, could not hear so many things, how could the whole people of Israel, composed of tailors, cooks, butchers, shepherds, slaves, and maids, to all of whom the law was handed down to be read, have borne the weight of all the Mosaic wisdom or, rather, of the whole divine wisdom? On the summit of that mountain, that very mountain on which the Lord often talked to the disciples, the face of the Prophet Moses, illuminated by the light of the divine sun, shone in a miraculous manner. But because the people with imperfect eyes, owl-like, could not stand the light, he used to address them with his face veiled.

But let us turn back to the Christians: Matthew was the first to write the Gospel and, as the prophet says, "hiding the word of God in his heart so that he might not sin,"[8] he pursued in his story only what pertained to the humanity of Christ, lest the memory of His deeds be lost in oblivion; therefore, we should understand Christ symbolized by man in the mystic spectacle of Ezekiel.[9] When the three Gospels had already been circulated and many years had passed since the crucifixion of the Lord on the cross, John, who revealed better than all the others the secrets of the Divinity, was compelled to say what he long had kept silent about the eternal generation of the Son, so that he might abolish the heresy of the Ebionites, who asserted Christ was man and not God. But he announced it obscurely in a few words, commencing thence: "In the beginning was the Word."[10]

Paul denies the Corinthians the true food, because they still live by the laws of the flesh and not of the spirit, and only before the elect he speaks the language of wisdom.[11] The disciple of Paul, Dionysius the Areopagite, writes that it was a prescribed and holy custom in the church not to communicate the most secret dogma in writing, but only by voice and to those who had been properly initiated.[12]

I have pursued this subject at length because there are many who, because they have drawn their argument from the rough appearance of the words, condemn and spurn the book of Moses as mediocre and trivial. And nothing is less credible to them than Moses' having anything more divine in depth than what he puts forth on the surface. If this has been sufficiently refuted, now it is easy to believe that if anywhere it was treated by him concerning the nature and the maker of the whole world, that is, if the treasures of the whole philosophical truth have been buried somewhere in his work as in a field, this has been done mostly in the past where assuredly and avowedly he philosophizes on the emanation of everything from God, and on the degree, the number, and the order of the parts of the world. On that account, there was a decree of the ancient Hebrews, which also Jerome mentioned, that no one, unless of mature age, should touch this account of the creation of the world.[13] Therefore, perhaps I will seem to have carried on a worthy endeavor if, after applying myself for a long time with exact care and great effort, so far as permitted through my weakness, I have pried into for study a discernment of the message of Moses.

But because I was aware that many Latins and Greeks had labored on this text, as well as the ancient Hebrews and Chaldean interpreters and an almost unlimited number of modern commentators, I scarcely dared to think of writing something new or of commenting on this subject. Yet, I remembered the stipulation of the Mosaic Law that no one should harvest completely his whole field but should leave a portion of it untouched for the poor and the needy, who might get there shocks and bundles to satisfy their hunger.[14] When this had come into mind, I began to glean with keen eyes the endless fields of the Prophet to see whether, since the very learned commentators were no less observers of the law than interpreters, they had in accordance with the edict of the law left some part untouched to be harvested by us less gifted. Whence also I might pluck for myself a few ears to place as first fruits of the crop upon the altars of the church so that I might not be deprived of the privileges of the temple like a false Israelite or someone uninitiated. From my offering it does not follow that I can, indeed, do anything which they could not do, but that they, because of the precept of the law, were unwilling to block the path of study of those to come. Besides, the vastness and fertility of the field is such that no number of harvesters can be equal to it even though they exerted all their strength on it with almost endless and most vigorous energy; however, I can still quote the saying that is in the Gospel: "Large harvest, few harvesters."[15]

Therefore, what has been written about this book by saintly men like Ambrose and Augustine, Strabo, Bede, and Remigius, and among the most recent ones by Aegidius and Albert, and written among the Greeks by Philo, Origen, Basil, Theodoretus, Apollinarius, Didymus, Diodorus, Severus, Eusebius, Josephus, Gennadius, and Chrysostom will be left out completely by me, because it is foolhardy and superfluous for a weak man to work in that part of the field where the most robust worked long ago. Likewise, I shall give no mention of what, in the Chaldean language, Jonathan, Anchelos, or the venerable Simeon handed down; or what the early Hebrews, Eleazar, Aba, John, Neonias, Isaac, and Joseph wrote, or, among the more recent ones, Gersonides, Sadias, Abraham, both Moseses, Solomon, and Manaem.

Besides all these, I shall introduce seven more expositions, my discoveries and meditations; in which expositions I shall take care first to overcome, if possible, three difficulties with which all who have undertaken to comment on this book seem to have had a great and difficult ordeal. The first one of the three difficulties is to prevent Moses from seeming to have spoken insufficiently or with too little learning and wisdom. Some released themselves from this charge, therefore, by saying that Moses did not speak about everything and did not reach grand and exalted heights because he was talking to naive people who were not capable of the understanding of every truth. We can believe there was satisfaction for the naive people if he offered the light of knowledge, that enlightens wise men but is hidden under popular terms, like under a shell, so that less-trained eyes would not be

19

blinded. Therefore, he was bringing the light to benefit healthy eyes, but he brought it hidden and veiled lest it hurt the bleary-eyed. He neither ought, nor could, nor wished to help the learned more than the unlearned.

The second difficulty is maintaining a constant interpretation criteria that would be coherent and, in itself, proper, and that would focus the entire range of ideas into only one line guided by a set plan toward that same meaning from which it started. If somewhere I introduce Moses talking perchance about ideas, in his next presentation I do not wish him to talk about the elements or about men. This kind of exposition is arbitrary and violent; nevertheless, to avoid it in the comment of this book has seemed, I do not say difficult, but really impossible for many and has appeared to all certainly laborious. How great the perplexity, the ambiguity, and the variety of the whole work is! See how great a labor I have conceived, (May I be equal to it!) which may not be easy to do, to interpret, without use of previous commentators, the whole creation of the world, not in one way but in seven ways, producing completely a new work from the beginning, continuous and free from confusion.

The third difficulty is concerned with this: that I not make the Prophet or the Holy Spirit through the Prophet assert anything unusual or prodigious, or alien to the nature of the things, as it is now seen, or alien to that truth ascertained by the better philosophers which even men of our own faith have accepted. Why then seven interpretations are offered by me, why I undertook to do them, what my plan was and what necessity drove me to them, and what this novelty is that I strive to bring about—I shall make clear in the following chapter.

In that chapter portraying the ideal man who was supposed to write so completely of the creation of the world as to emulate nature itself, I shall try to prove that actually our Prophet never fell short of that ideal as an archetype. On the contrary, he followed it in all respects so that no one else should be proposed as such an ideal, and we can all admire his greatness more readily than evaluate his merits.

These works of mine, such as they are, the first attempt of my youth so far, are offered to you, most noble Lorenzo, because they are mine and I dedicated and devoted myself to you a long time ago, and because you offered me the retreat in Fiesole, where they were born.

This retreat which has also been enlivened by the frequent, I should say continuous, visits of your friend Angelo Poliziano, whose pleasant and fertile mind, I think, now promises a fruit of philosophy as important and mature as, in the past, his literary flowers were varied. One might add, it is the custom to congratulate those we love and respect when something festive or joyful happens, not only to congratulate them with words, but also with some gift to add to their happiness and, as I have thus said, make a joyful witness to them of our affection.

Most timely, therefore, my work of nocturnal study comes to you in the time in which your son Giovanni, at an unprecedented age, has been destined by the Supreme Pontiff Innocent VIII for the topmost college of Christian orders, both for his natural characteristics which promise all good things and for your own merits and authority, demanding it rightly and justly for him. It remains that I hope he may show himself deserving of his honor. He will do this if he takes as his model him who has been both his father and promoter of this honor, a model that is of all wisdom and all virtue. Farewell.

SECOND FOREWORD OF THE WHOLE WORK

The ancients conceived three worlds. The highest of all is the ultra mundane or supercelestrial one, which the theologians call "angelic" and the philosophers call "intelligible" and which by no one, Plato said in the *Phaedrus*,[1] has ever been worthily described. Next to this is the celestial world. Last is this sublunar world which we inhabit. The latter is the world of darkness; the first world is of light; the celestial world is composed of light and darkness. This former world is characterized by water, a fluid and unstable substance; the latter world is characterized by fire, because of the splendor of its light and the height of its position; the celestial is in the middle and, therefore, is called by the Hebrews "Asciamaim," as if it were composed of fire and water which I have already mentioned. Here is a succession of life and death; there, eternal life and never-ending activity; in the celestial world, a succession of activity and positions.

This terrestial [sublunar] world is made of the perishable substance of the physical bodies; the intelligible world [ultra-mundane] is made of the divine nature of the mind; and the celestial world is constituted of body, but incorruptible, and of the mind, but subject to the body. The third world is moved by the second; and the second is ruled by the first; and among them there are a great many differences which here it is not the plan to enumerate where I skim the surface rather than fathom the depths.

But I should not pass over the fact that these three worlds were fashioned very clearly by Moses in the construction of his admirable

22

tabernacle. In fact, he divided the tabernacle into three parts, whose single parts could in no way more expressly represent the corresponding worlds which I described. The first part, protected by no roof or cover was open and exposed to the rain, the snow, the sun, the heat, and the cold; and what fits evidently the image of our sublunar world, not only pure and impure, sacred and secular men inhabit it, but also animals of all kinds; and in it (the first part) was also the endless succession of life and death because of the offerings and living sacrifices. The remaining two parts were protected everywhere from foreign attacks just as the celestial and super-celestial worlds are susceptible to neither injury nor offense. Both parts likewise were honored with a title of holiness but in such a way that the more secret one was honored by the title of Holy of Holies and the other simply Holy; just as, although both the celestial and angelic worlds are holy because after the fall of Lucifer there neither is nor can be any mishap or sin above the moon, the angelic world, however, is considered far more sacred and divine than the celestrial world.

But why do I pursue these remote resemblances? If the last part of the tabernacle was common to men and animals, the second, which was all shining with the splendor of gold, was illuminated by a candelabra of seven lamps, which as all the Latin, Greek, and Hebrew interpreters indicate, signify the seven planets. In the third part, the most sacred of all, were the winged Cherubims. Does not this place the three worlds before our eyes? This world which both men and animals inhabit; the celestial world, where the planets shine; and the super-celestial, the habitation of the angels.

From here I am reminded also of the highest Sacrament of the Gospel. Since through the Crucifixion and blood of Christ there was unlocked for us the way to the super-celestial world, to communion with the angels; therefore, in the moment of His [Christ's] death, the veil of the temple was rent asunder, the veil by which the Holy of Holies, through which as I have said the angelic world is signified, was separated from the rest. This was a sign that to man there lay open access to the kingdom of God and to God Himself, Who flies above the Cherubim—that access originally closed by decree of the Divine Law because of the sin of the first father.

This is enough concerning the three worlds about which it must be especially observed—a fact on which my intention almost wholly depends—that the three worlds are only one, not solely because all are related by a single beginning and to the same end, or because, regulated by defined laws, they are connected to each other by a harmonious natural bond and by an ordinary series of steps; but because whatever is in all of the worlds is at the same time also contained in each, and there is no one of them in which there are not all properties which are in each of the others. If I understood him correctly, this, I believe, was the opinion of Anaxagoras—also expressed by the Pythagoreans and by the Platonists.[2] Therefore, whatever is in the lower worlds is also in the higher ones, but in a more refined (superior) form; similarly, what is found in the higher worlds can be seen also in the lower ones, but in a deteriorated condition and with a somewhat adulterated nature, so to speak. Among us, heat is an elemental quality: in the celestial world it is a calorific power [virtue]; in the angelic minds, it is an idea of warmth. I shall speak more clearly: among us, fire is a physical element; the sun is fire in the sky, the celestial world; in the region above man, fire is the seraphic intellect. But see how they differ: the elemental fire burns, the celestial fire enlivens, the super-celestial fire loves. Water is among us: in the celestial world there is the water which is mover and mistress of this world, namely the moon, vestibule of the heavens; and the waters above the heavens are the cherubic minds. But see what a disparity of condition occurs in the same nature: the basic moisture surfeits the heat of life, the celestial one nourishes it, and the super-celestial one understands it.

In the first world, God, Primal Unity, presides over nine orders of angels as if over as many spheres and, while motionless, moves all toward Himself. In the middle world, that is, the celestial one, the Empyrean, in the same manner as a leader presides over his army, presides over the nine celestial spheres, each of the spheres revolving in continuous motion; the Empyrean, nevertheless, imitating God remains still. In the elementary world, after the prime matter, its foundation, there are nine spheres of corruptible forms. Three of them are bodies without life, which are the elements and the mixtures; then midway between them are those things which are mixed but also imperfect, like atmospheric phenomena, which occur in the sky.

Three are of vegetable nature, which is divided into the three primary genders of herbs, bushes, and trees. Three are of sensitive souls, which are imperfect as in the zoophytes, or even perfect but within the limits of the irrational phantasy: that which is highest in the brute, capable of erudition of man, a mean, for instance, in between brute and man as the zoophyte is a mean between brute and plant.

But concerning these facts, this work is more than enough. I add only this much: the mutual harmony of the worlds has been written also in the Scriptures, both when it is written in the *Psalms*: "He Who creates the celestial levels by understanding. . . ."[3] and we read that the angels of God are spirits, and His ministers are a flame of burning fire.[4]

Hence, often to the divine are given celestial and even earthly names which are sometimes represented by stars, wheels and animals, or by elements. Thus celestial names are often given to earthly things.[5] In fact, held together by ties of harmony, all these worlds with mutual liberality exchange their natures as well as their names. From this principle, in case anyone has not yet understood it, came the discipline of all allegoric interpretation. The ancient fathers could have not represented some things with some images and other things with other images unless instructed, as I have accordingly said, into the hidden relationships and affinities of the whole of nature. Otherwise, there would be no reason why they represented this thing by this image and another by another, rather than each by the opposite of that image. But skilled in all things and moved by that Spirit, Which not only knows the universe but created it, the ancient fathers represented very skillfully the natures of one world through those which they knew corresponded to them in other worlds. Therefore, those who want to interpret correctly figures and allegorical senses (unless the same spirit is also at hand) are in need of the same knowledge.

However, there is, besides those three I mentioned, a fourth world in which are found all these things which are in the other worlds. This is man himself, who, for this reason, as the Catholic teachers say, is referred to in the Gospel by the name of every creature, when it is said that the Gospel must be preached to all men not to brutes and the angels; nevertheless, it is demanded by Christ that it be preached to every creature.[6] In the schools it is a common saying that man is a lesser world in which is seen a body composed of elements, and the celestial spirit, and the vegetal soul of the plants, and the sensitivity of the brutes, and reason, and the angelic mind, and the image of God.

Therefore, if I assume these four worlds, it is credible that Moses, going to speak exhaustively concerning the universe, should have discoursed about all these things; and since a writer will imitate nature, if he is a consultant of nature, as I believe this writer of ours was if anyone ever was, it is conceivable that his doctrine about the worlds was arranged not differently from the way God, the Omnipotent Maker, arranged them in themselves, so that actually this scripture of Moses is the true image of the universe, just as we also read that on the mountain where he learned these things he was instructed to do everything following the example which he had seen on the mountain.[7]

Accordingly, the first principle, which, as I have shown, is the greatest of all, is that those things that are in all worlds are contained in each. Moses, as an imitator of nature, had to deal with each of the worlds in such a way as to deal equally with all of them using the same word in the same context. From this springs a four-fold exposition of the whole Mosaic text, so that, in the first place, whatever is written there I interpret on the angelic and invisible world, making no mention of the other worlds. In the second place, I interpret everything with respect to the celestial world; then, with respect to the sublunary and corruptible one; in the fourth place, with respect to the nature of man. In fact, if anywhere there will be investigated, for instance, the intelligible world, because it contains in itself all the lower natures, the same scriptures may advise us about other worlds; surely we can or we ought by all means to interpret all the particulars about all the worlds.

In turn, although the various natures are enclosed mutually by each other, they, nevertheless, have been allotted particular abodes and certain unique powers. Accordingly, although in the various parts of the present work the four-fold aspects of the universe are treated in the same order as the scriptures, it must be believed, nevertheless, that in the first part more particularly the first nature is discussed, and in succession the others in the same order.

From this springs the need for a fifth version. It is added because these natures are different; nevertheless, there is no multiplicity which is not a unit, and the parts are tied together by a certain discordant agreement and bound by multiform chains. Because it is probable that Moses did this throughout the whole work, I am pushed, even if unwillingly, toward a sixth exposition. In it I shall show that there are fifteen different ways in which we can understand one thing as tied or linked to another thing; and since there are neither more nor less than fifteen, all these ways have been expressed so sufficiently and distinctly by the Prophet that Aristotle has never written anything more clearly on the nature of things.

Finally, as the Sabbath, or a rest, follows the six days of creation, it is proper also for me, after dealing with the orders of things which emanate from God and explaining their unity and diversity, their ties and practices, to touch on a seventh or sabbatical exposition, which may be called sabbatical, an interpretation of the joy of the creatures and their return to God, which through Mosaic and Christian Law was granted to men long rejected because of the fault of the first father. I shall reveal in this present work what Moses clearly hid so that it might be publicly read concerning the advent of Christ, the development of the Church, and the calling of the Gentiles. So truly this book, probably the only one of this kind, is characterized by seven seals, and is full of the whole wisdom, of all the mysteries.

Moreover, I shall not imitate those who have tried at some time to present this creation of the world. They have put in their work everything worthy considering God, the Angels, the matter, the sky, and all nature that has been discussed so far among philosophers and theologians. Among the Hebrews, Isaac Persa and Samual Ophinides have especially transgressed. I shall only try to clarify, relative to my abilities, what the Mosaic scripture means and what the context indicates or signifies. As an example, if I show that the firmament means the eighth sphere, I shall not discuss immediately the way it moves the other spheres, or how many signs and images identify the eighth sphere, or whether or not it is turned with a simple motion or rather with two or three motions. In the same way, if somewhere I mentioned that the soul of man is identified with a certain name then I shall not relate everything that has been said on the soul, but on every subject I shall only note briefly and rapidly the things the author seems explicitly to mention.

I have said "briefly" and "rapidly" because it is not the intention of this work to be such that those who have not learned these things somewhere else will learn them here for the first time, but that they may recognize in the words of the Prophet what they know already to be true, and that by understanding how the legislator Moses gathered and indicated here in a few words truths they have read presented in a multitude of books by philosophers and theologians, they may now listen to the lawgiver speaking with unveiled face.

Then, if anyone prompted perhaps by a spirit of holy simplicity does not even approve these mysteries probed so deeply but rather desires a simpler and more accepted explanation of the holy text, I shall bid him to remember Paul's precept, that he who eateth shall not despise him that eateth not and that he that eateth not should not judge him that eateth.[8] Then I shall address him not with my words but with those of Augustine in his own exposition of *Genesis*, in this manner: "If you can, do learn these things, if you cannot, leave them to your betters. Profit from a book which does not abandon your weakness and which with a motherly step walks slowly along with you; for it speaks thus to mock the proud with its loftiness, to terrify the studious with its profundity, to feed the great with its truth, to sustain the humble with its courtesy."[9] But let us come back to ourselves and starting from the same corruptible world which we inhabit, let me accomplish so far as possible what I have promised. Otherwise "In great endeavors it is sufficient to have tried"[10] and, as says Pomerius, "A great effort is the beginning of great things."[11]

MOSES' WORDS TO BE EXPOUNDED

These are the Prophet's very words which I undertake to interpret.

In the beginning God created heaven and earth. And the earth was void and empty, and darkness was upon the face of the deep, and the Spirit of God moved over the waters. And God said: "Let there be light." And light was made. And God saw the light that it was good; and he divided the light from the darkness. He called the light day and the darkness night, and the evening and the morning were the first day. And God said: "Let there be a firmament in the midst of the waters and let it divide the waters from the waters." And God made a firmament, and divided the waters that were under the firmament from the waters that were above the firmament. And it was so. And God called the firmament heaven. And the evening and the morning were the second day. And God said: "Let all the waters under the heaven be gathered into one place and let the dry land appear." And it was so done. And God called the dry land earth, and the gathering together of the waters He called Seas. And God saw that it was good. And He said: "Let the earth bring forth the green herb yielding seeds and fruit tree yielding fruit whose seeds will be according to its kind." And it was done. And the earth brought forth the green herb yielding seed according to its kind. And God saw that it was good. And the evening and the morning were the third day. And God said: "Let there be lights in the firmament of heaven to divide the day from the night and let them be for signs and for seasons and for days, and years, to shine in the firmament of heaven and illuminate the earth.'' And it was so done. And God, therefore, made two great lights, a greater light to rule the day and a lesser light to rule the night, and the stars. And He set them in the firmament of heaven to shine upon the earth, and to rule the day and night and to divide the light and darkness. And God saw that this was good. And the evening and the morning were the fourth day. And God also said: ''Let the water produce the creeping creatures having life and fowls that may fly over the earth under the firmament of heaven.'' And God created the great whales and every living and moving creature, which the waters produced according to their kinds, and every winged fowl according to its kind. And God saw that this was good. And he blessed them saying: ''Increase and multiply and fill the waters of the seas; and let the birds be multiplied upon the earth.'' And the evening and the morning were the fifth day. And God said: ''Let the earth bring forth the living creature in its kind, cattle and creeping things, and beasts of the earth, according to their kinds.'' And this was done. And God made the beasts of the earth according to their kinds, and cattle and everything that creepeth on the earth after its kind. And God saw that it was good. And He said: ''Let us make man to our image and likeness; and let him have dominion over the fishes of the sea, and the fowls of the air, and the beasts, and the whole earth, and every creeping creature that moveth upon the earth.'' And God created man to His own image; to the image of God He created him.[1]

Thus far I have undertaken to expound Moses. I have divided the whole exposition into seven books or treatises, more to imitate Basil and Augustine than because the reader's close attention may be revived by a frequent pause. Additionally, since the seven expositions are divided in seven books and the seven books in seven chapters, all correspond to the seven days of creation. By a very consistent plan, it has been arranged by me that, just as the seventh day in the writings of Moses is the Sabbath, or the day of rest, so every one of my expositions intentionally closes with a seventh chapter on Christ, Who is the end of the law, our Sabbath, our rest, and our happiness.

FIRST EXPOSITION: OF THE ELEMENTARY WORLD

First Chapter of the First Book

The naturalistic philosophers, who examine the nature of corruptible things, agree in general about their origins as follows: that there is crude matter without form but, although deprived of all forms because of its nature, capable of assuming them all.

Therefore, besides matter, the philosophers make privation the origin of natural things. Averroes[1] added that matter is expanded to three dimensions: length, width, depth; so that corporeal things might not be said to be derived from an incorporeal subject. The philosophers then introduce the cause of change which they call the "efficient," by whose force when matter, which is potentiality, is molded, occasionally becomes actual, just as soft and shapeless wax molded and wielded by the hands is transformed into different forms at the will of the molder. And because nature does not do anything by mere chance, but always for the sake of pursuing something good, instantly the "final cause" presents itself and the nearest end of the acting cause is the form which it draws from the heart of the matter. In fact, the former intentionally directs and keeps turning the matter to bring it to a perfect state of form. This is why Aristotle[2] set form as the third principle. However, it can not be taken out solely from the heart of the matter unless the matter is first prepared and endowed with harmonious qualities; around which all the effort of the creator and all the activity of the creator is consumed until, suddenly, in an instant, the species shines as reward of the deed.

The Peripatetics call the Creator himself a "cause" rather than a "principle." The divine Platonics, always mindful of divine things, want us reminded that even if the natural agents seem to us to be the only one to move, form, and change the bodies, they are not really the primary cause of what happens but rather instruments of the divine act which they obey and assist. Likewise, although the hands of the craftsman are the ones which compose, arrange, and transmute all the materials of a house—stones, wood, cement—and nothing else besides them seems attending to the construction of the house; however, we know that the craftsman's hands, as a docile tool, assist that art, which established in the mind of the architect, simultaneously conceives, carries out in all the details, and realizes the planning of the house in the insensitive matter. This is the way the Platonics conceive two causes: organic and exemplary. And the Peripatetics would not deny this, but prove this by the old saying among them that "every deed of nature is a deed of intelligence."

This is what usually is said of corruptible things, all of which Moses so included in the work of the first day that concerning these things the most reknowned philosophers have spoken nothing more certainly nor more aptly.

Second Chapter

Thus, at the beginning he places two causes: the acting cause and the material cause, namely, the potentiality and the actuality. He calls the former one "heaven" and the latter one "earth"; our interpretation is first confirmed by the authority of the Stoics, who call "heaven" the acting cause and "earth" the material cause, as Varro,[3] not to mention the Greeks, writes. Reason also proves this. In fact, matter is the lowest of all natural conditions, as earth is of all elements; and the relationship of the acting cause with the matter is identical to that relationship of the heaven to the earth, as the Peripatetics have proven. The earth, moreover, is "empty" and "bare" substance, as

32

Jerome has interpreted it, or "invisible" and "disorderly," according to the Septuagint.[4] All these qualities apply to the rough and shapeless matter which, lacking all form, is rightly considered empty and without shape and which is wholly irregular and invisible. But the Hebrew words "tou" and "bou," which are read at this point, are interpreted differently by many Hebrews. For example, they interpret "tou" as brutal, stupefying, and astonishing, which is related to the dark and deformed appearance of matter because it leaves us, straining for knowledge of this, astounded. For this reason, Aristotle said it is known by us through an analogy and, according to Plato, through unfounded reason.[5]

Because of the force of the word, however, many interpret "bou" as the beginning and rudiment of form. In fact, literally, to say "bou" is the same thing as saying, "there is in it" or "there is something in it." Following this interpretation, we shall understand the rudimentary form of substance, as well as its potentiality, to be in the earth. Not only did Albertus Magnus[6] and many Peripatetics believe this, but also the ancient Hebrews, as we clearly learn from the testimony of the ancient Simeon. But Moses explains how this beginning of form should be interpreted, adding: "And the darkness was over the face of the deep." He calls the earth "the deep," that is, the matter extended boundlessly in three dimensions. Above this was darkness, namely privation, a well-known principle among the Peripatetics and whose most appropriate name is darkness. In fact, privation as it differs from negation, Albertus Magnus always maintains, is this same beginning of form about which we are speaking and about which the same philosopher has argued copiously and subtly.

Furthermore, if the earth is below the waters which irrigate it, and when irrigated by them conceives what later it spawns, will not the waters in this case signify the accidental qualities and dispositions of matter? Either by their flow or their fluid nature these have the aspect of waters by which, as I thus said, moistened matter conceives the form which, at the last moment of its time, it brings forth into light. Upon these waters the Spirit of the Lord, namely, the power and the efficient cause, the organ and the instrument of the Lord, is rightfully said to be borne. It is not said that the Spirit of the Lord is borne upon the earth because its action does not touch or penetrate the subject except through the medium of its qualities. While it turns and puts these in motion, a light, that is the beauty and the splendor of the form, rises, and puts to flight the above-mentioned darkness, namely, privation. And this occurs with the voice of God commanding, since the natural causes do nothing which the order of divine art has not preordained.

In this way from the morning and the evening was made one day, because from the nature of potential and actuality bursts asunder a third substance which we call composite; and now, following this interpretation, the reason is clear why he said "one day" and not "the first day"; and he rightly saw the light because it was good, since the nature of the form is only a pale image and a shady copy of the primal good. Here is what generally can be said of the corruptible matter below the moon where we see both heaven and earth, namely, the transmuting nature and that which is transmuted, and where we see the earth itself, that is, matter void of every kind of substance and, likewise, free from all accidental form; and above the earth, extending into the three-dimensional abysses, we see the brooding darkness of privation, not inside the earth (in fact, as Aristotle says, privation is not the essence of matter),[7] but a covering on its external surface.

Likewise, we see that the Spirit of the Lord is borne above the waters, that is, on the fluid tendencies present in matter as in earth. The Spirit of the Lord expresses the power of active cause, not as principal cause. As the Spirit of God is the instrument of the divine art, in the same manner our vital spirit is the instrument of the soul. And at once, by the order of God the Maker, with the Spirit acting on those waters and motivating the substance, the light, that is the splendor and the beauty of the form, arose.

Third Chapter

But because from common and general principles I descend in proper order to particulars, as Aristotle proves,[8] so does Moses: after he has spoken about these things which are common to all elementary principles, on the second day he divides into three aspects the whole of the elementary substance. However, first it must be understood that he designates all the material forms here by the name ''waters,'' a term which could not be more fitting. In fact, matter is like the bed of the sea; in this sphere of generable and corruptible things, there is a perpetual flux of forms coming and going as the ebb and flow of the tide.

That is, as Solomon says, ''generation passeth away and generation cometh, but earth abideth forever'';[9] hence these forms are called by the Platonists, always imitators of Hebraic wisdom, generations instead of forms, because they can more truly be said to become than to be.

Moreover, for this reason Moses, who precedently called the quantities and accidental forms of matter by the name of ''waters,'' would call material substances themselves by the same name here also; in other words, this is done to remind us that qualities are certainly not the same essential forms of the elements, as Alexander[10] believed they were; but, as the Platonists confirmed with great effort, every species which is in matter should be referred to as the condition of accident rather than as true substance. Those things rightfully claim the latter title for themselves, which stand up on their own, supported by themselves, and which are with true reasoning what they are, unmixed and the least adulterated with foreign matters. Heraclitus called the sea the substance of sensible things, and the poets, hiding philosophy behind a veily myth, divided the perceptible world into three parts. After the unitary rule of Saturn (that is, after the union of the intelligible world encompassing everything within itself), they ascribed the celestial region to Jupiter, the subterranean one to Pluto, and the middle region which extends from the moon to the earth, with which we are now dealing, to Neptune, the Lord of the sea, who for that quality is considered among the Platonists to preside over the generations.[11]

Now let us refer to Moses' dividing the waters from the waters with the firmament. In fact, the division of sublunar bodies is trifold. Some are above the middle region of the atmosphere, namely, the highest part of this element and the purest fire which usually is designated by

35

the name of ether: there are the pure and unmixed elements governed by laws. Below the middle part of the air are other bodies, which exist among us, where there is no pure element (not even a pure sensitive element), but all things are mixtures composed of the dregs and crasser part of the world's body.

Intervening in the region of the air, which is here called "firmament," from whence come, as Moses says, the birds flying below the firmament of heaven, is the region in which appear certain celestial phenomena: rain, snow, lightning, thunder, comets, and the like. See now how rightly this firmament, not only because of its position but also because of its natural qualities, divides and distinguishes the superior from the inferior elements, like the waters from the waters.

Above it are the pure elements; below it, in a perfect mixture, they abandon their elementary simplicity. Within it they are mixed but imperfect and, to speak with absolute correctness, mediocre, between the nature of mixtures and elements.

Fourth Chapter

But let us see what else Moses philosophizes: "Let the waters that are under the heavens be gathered together in one place," He orders, "and let dry earth appear." Dry earth, as I established before, is matter, and matter neither appears nor is seen unless dressed in the semblance of forms, but it does not appear dressed with the semblance of an element because, as I said and as the philosophers prove, the simple element can neither be seen, nor touched, nor fall wholly under any sense. Therefore, if the earth which was formerly invisible is going to become visible, it is necessary for the waters located below the heavens, that is under the middle region of the air, to be collected into only one place, or, in other words, that they merge in a single common mixture according to certain laws, as if prescribed by lictors.

What happens to the lower waters as I have shown does not happen to the higher ones, where the mixture is nonexistent or imperfect. But if the vegetative soul immediately follows upon the form of the mixture, what else did we expect from our philosopher but that, after the converging of the waters, he would immediately tell about the earth fertile with herbs, fruits and trees?

Fifth Chapter

Although it might seem that henceforth following in order, Moses ought to proceed to the animals whose kind of soul is next to the vegetative; nevertheless, because from animals one goes on to man in whom all treatment of the perishable world ends, Moses, for this reason, inserted some reflections about those things that are produced in the firmament and about those things by which it [the firmament] is adorned, just as the earth is adorned by what is produced in it: metals, plants, animals. These are the phenomena [of the firmament] produced high in the middle region of the air. Previously Moses called this both "heaven" and "firmament," here, instead, it is called the "firmament of the heaven" to let us know that it is not truly heaven but what is below heaven. For this reason, Ennius in *Achilles* called this part "subiices,"[12] as it is placed immediately below heaven. That these phenomena are called by the philosophers secondary stars and heavenly bodies and constellations is too well known to be proved at length or to seem surprising to anyone that I not explain those facts which are said here with respect to stars. Whereas all diversity in these is due to two prime causes, warmth and cold, there is a good reason for my ascribing what is caused by warmth to the sun and ascribing what is caused by the cold to the moon. These phenomena claim for themselves the names of the sun, the moon, and of other heavenly bodies, not only because they are the same in the lower heaven as those in the more divine heaven, or because with a similar look, equally bright and shining, they appear to men, but because some of them follow certain heavenly bodies in the heavens as a master and a guide. Therefore, they are also signs of those things by which the heavenly bodies have usually been stimulated to portend to men below. To prove it, there is the fact that they follow the movement of the heavenly bodies by whose strength and influence they subsist from prepared terrestrial matter, that is, from vaporous exhalations.

Sixth Chapter

Now is clear what follows about the creation of animals and men. In fact, after the plants there are those hybrids which have sense and motion, although the Pythagoreans ascribe also to the plants an unconscious sensitivity.[13] I shall discuss this in that concordance,[14] a work of more detailed analysis I am bringing out. Then, animals, which without controversy participate in sense and motion, are divided, both here by Moses and in the *Timaeus*[15] into the volatile, aquatic, and terrestrial ones. First and highest of all species is man, and having reached him, the nature of the corruptible world pauses and orders a signal of retreat.

Seventh Chapter

As man is the absolute consummation of all lower species, so Christ is the supreme consummation of all men. Therefore, if, as the philosophers say, from what in each species is the supreme perfection, perfection is drawn off, as from a spring, to the others of the same kind; it is doubtful to no one that the perfection of all good in all men is derived from the man, Christ. To Him only has Spirit without measure been given so that we might receive everything from His fullness. See, without doubt, how much this prerogative is due to Him as man and God, which also, in His capacity as man, is peculiar to Him and belongs to Him as a legitimate privilege.

SECOND EXPOSITION: OF THE
CELESTIAL WORLD

Proemium

From the elements let us now rise to the heavens, from corruptible
to incorruptible bodies, so that it may be clear to everyone that in the
same words in which there has been shown so much about the
elementary nature, there has also been included by the Prophet sublime dogmas about the celestial nature. After pondering this, another
theory besides that one indicated in the proems will appear evident to
us. Why, for example, when Moses was going to speak about active
cause and about matter, did he not in precise words call the former
"active" and the latter "matter," in place of "heaven" and "earth"?
And, why did he call the compositions of matter not "qualities," as
the philosophers say, but "waters"? And why did he call form
"light" instead of "form"? And likewise, why did he not call
comets, lightning, and similar phenomena by their proper names
instead of "heavenly bodies" and "stars," and so on concerning the
other things?

In the proems, indeed, I pointed out not only the custom of the
ancients of writing about great natural and divine things occultly and
figuratively but also the ignorance of the hearers: who, because they
could not stand the splendor of the Mosaic wisdom, were properly
addressed with a veiled face [metaphorically], lest those intended to

be illuminated would not be blinded by the excessive brightness. Now I have the occasion for a third explanation; namely, that if Moses had called "matter" and "form" and "quality" and "acting cause" by these names, they could have been used to discuss the corruptible world, to be sure, but not the others. Therefore, it is a contrived and wonderful artifice of Moses, fitting truly divine not human ability, to use the same names and to structure his presentation in a way that the same words, same context, and same sequence in the whole passage are perfectly fitted for symbolizing the secrets of all worlds and of the whole of nature. And, it is at this very point that the book of Moses surpasses all human knowledge in doctrine, eloquence, and genius.

This is the new and heretofore untouched aspect that I have tried to illuminate in order to show my contemporaries, by the facts themselves, what Moses did.

This is the model, this is the example of the unsurpassable writer. Not only because, as I have shown above, does such a style reproduce and emulate nature, but also because, as among the angelic minds, following the authority of Dionysius and of St. Thomas,[1] the light of our theology, that one is the most advanced who by intelligence comprehends with fewest notions and forms what is embraced by the inferior minds with various and numerous notions. Thus, among the scriptures the one which is supreme and stays at the height of all perfections is that one which in very few words embraces things logically and profoundly in their wholeness as in their individual parts. But why hold back any longer the Prophet who is coming forward with unveiled expression to speak to us about the celestial mysteries? However, before we hear him speak, it will be better to present a few modest thoughts about the tenth heaven so that we may be more capable of understanding his words.

First Chapter

Above the nine celestial circles, namely the seven planets, the eighth sphere, which is called that of the fixed stars, and the ninth sphere, which is comprehended by reason, not by sense, and which is first among the moving bodies, there is believed to exist a tenth sphere, steady and motionless because it does not participate in any movement. This has been believed not only by our very recent scholars as Strabo and Bede,[2] but also by many Hebrews and, furthermore, by certain philosophers and mathematicians. Let it suffice to mention two of them: the eminent Spanish astrologer Abraam, and the philosopher Isaac, both of whom attest this.[3] Actually, Isaac believes the tenth sphere to be what Ezekiel designated as the sapphire in the likeness of a throne because the color of the sapphire signifies the splendor of its light and the similarity to a throne signifies its immobility. Likewise, as Zacaria, he believes the ten spheres to be symbolized by the seven-branched golden candelabra, the lamp above it, and the two olive trees above the lamp.[4] Since the seven candelabra branches indicate the seven planets, and the lamp indicates the eighth sphere shining with so many lights, he wants the ninth and tenth spheres to be indicated by the two olive trees, because it is from the olives that the oil flows as nourishment to the lamp and branches of the candlestick. Through a similarity of pattern, since the light of the heaven we see emanates and is maintained from the highest heavens (for what gives light also maintains it), the latter are deservingly likened to the olives, and the former, to the candlestick and lamp.

But, if two primary sources cannot be assigned to the same water, one of those two spheres must be the first principle of all the light. And, if light is traced back to one sphere as to its source, namely, to the tenth, which becomes then the unifying principle of light, thence the ninth sphere may first receive the light with all the essence of its substance. Thirdly, from here, it may come to the sun with full participation, and then fourthly, from the sun to the last step, it may be divided among all the stars. Therefore, let us establish above the nine celestial spheres, the tenth one which the philosophers call the "empyrean."

Some have doubted whether its nature was corporeal or incorporeal. In fact, it helps the unity if it corresponds by an analogy of nature to the elemental number, without being of the same kind. Whatever is concluded on this question, let it remain unshaken that in that place [tenth sphere] are the treasures of light, and that from it, just as from a primal fountain, whatever light is held and beheld in bodies is derived. And it is immaterial whether or not anyone wishes to believe more stubbornly than truly that the tenth sphere or empyrean is not of corporeal nature, because in the theology of the Phoenecians, as Caesar Julian writes in his oration on the sun,[5] it is believed that the corporeal light emanates from an incorporeal nature. Therefore, this tenth sphere governs the nine celestial regions coming under it in successive levels, as the general guides his army, as form shapes matter; and bearing the image of unity, it completes the row of ten.

Second Chapter

But, let us come back to Moses who, preparing to discuss them all [the celestial spheres], deemed this sphere as the first and most important, particularly worthy of the name "heaven." In the same way we can call the nine angelic choirs "gods" because they participate in the Divinity, and from this comes the expression "God of gods." However, when we say God in an absolute sense we do not mean one of them but the Indivisible Trinity which presides over them as the empyrean heaven presides over the nine orbits subordinated to it.

Moreover, Moses called the eight lowest spheres "earth," and not without reason, but on account of the fact that the extremes of this group assume for themselves the name of earth. They are the moon and the starry heaven, both of which by the authority of the ancients as well as our reason, we are compelled to call earth. In fact, it was very common in the Academy to name earth the eighth circle. Likewise Aristotle, undoubtedly imitating the Pythagoreans, who call it heavenly earth or earthly heaven, considered the moon similar to the earth.[6] But now you see what reasons lead us to both conclusions. In fact, if we examine the parts of the sky, we would consider as earth the moon, which is the lowest of all the heavenly bodies—just as the earth is the lowest and most ignoble of all the elements—and is very similar to the earth in the opacity of its substance and the presence of its defects. So, the water is Mercury, a shifting and changing planet and, therefore, called the orbiter of the waves by Lucan; the air is Venus, vivifying with temperate warmth; the fire is Sun for very evident reasons.

And in reverse order, Mars is fire; Jupiter, air connected by its nature to Venus; Saturn, water that is aged by an unconquerable coldness. It remains for us to name earth the eighth circle and unwandering sphere [that of fixed stars], this being required by the very order of the computation. Rightly, therefore, Moses called earth this aggregate over which there is nothing visible to us and which is enclosed on either hand by two earths. Then he adds: "And the Earth was void and empty," certainly because of the absence of light which was not coming yet from the first heaven and for the absence of other powers of which light is a vehicle.

I am not saying this on my own, but the author Moses himself states what is lacking, as he adds: "And darkness was on the surface of the deep," rightly calling "the deep" the great and exceptional altitudes of so many spheres. But, lest we believe that nothing is between the eighth circle and the seat of the empyrean, as many have believed who were following simply the indications of the senses, Moses reminds us of the middle orb which he himself symbolized by the waters, but which is aptly called crystalline heaven by more recent scholars. Over this was borne or, as the Hebrew wisdom has it and as Ephraim the Syrian translated it, "brooded" the Spirit of the Lord—that is, the closely adhering spiritual Olympus, the house of the Spirit of the Lord, warmed by its vivifying light.[7] And appropriately it occurs that that which holds closest to the origin of light, with all its body and all its weight, should absorb the light, which is invisible to us because it is not restrained by a more solid body.

So, in the beginning the brooding empyrean was bestowing upon that sphere its own light which, after darkness had been cast out at God's command, was soon spread to the other spheres which I have designated as the earth and the deep; and the evening and morning made one day since through the reception of light and supernal influence the lower heavens were joined with the first ones. To summarize, with the first day both the superiority of the first heaven over the others and the transference of light from it to them are briefly indicated, and by the names of water and earth the numerous characteristics of the ninth sphere and of the others are indicated.

Third Chapter

But now, speaking of the moving orbs more particularly, Moses teaches us that the sphere of the fixed stars which we call firmament is between two waters. The reason for this statement is evident from what I have said. In fact, as I said before, both the ninth sphere and the planet Saturn deserve to be called waters. The firmament was then placed by God in the midst of waters, and all the waters existing under the sky were gathered in one place. And it was arranged in such a way that "dry land" might appear, that is, the earth; and all of this was done for the welfare of all living creatures.

Consider what Moses meant with these words. The waters which are under the heavens are the seven heavenly bodies, of which the first is Saturn, which is under the firmament Moses called "heaven." These waters were gathered into only one place because all the power of the planets is collected solely in the sun. All philosophers and all mathematicians unanimously confirm this. If this mass of waters has been called "sea," quite likely will it be that Ocean which is conceived to be father of gods and men by those who honored the planets with names of gods.

And what else can we call earth other than the moon, so named by Aristotle and the Pythagoreans? That moon, which when it is all covered by the waves of the previously mentioned sea, is neither useful nor visible to us; but when by the progressive movement of the sea it comes more and more into view, it then becomes useful to the animals and to us. Then become fertile and fruitful those things especially of a vegetable nature, whose primary functions are growth, nourishment, and generation. As mentioned by the Chaldeans, the particular power of the moon is seen in these things. And this is demonstrated very openly by Moses when he introduces it as the principle whose appearance makes it the generator of grasses, fruits, and trees. See how he briefly sketched for us the nature of the moon and of the sun.

But why is he silent about the others when I promise in the proems that he will speak sufficiently and knowledgeably about everything? Why, I say, does he not say a word about the four remaining heavenly bodies, namely, Venus, Mercury, Jupiter, and Mars, while making mention of the tenth, the ninth, and the eighth spheres and also Saturn, the Sun, and the Moon? You will say perhaps he did it because those primitive people knew only the sun and the moon. But I closed this way out to myself and cannot use this explanation without blushing since I have already stated that Moses omitted nothing that might give perfect understanding of all the worlds. Let someone say that what he presented about the Sun and the Moon he has presented for the others, because these two heavenly bodies hold dominion over the heavens and exert a universal influence, while the power of the other planets is limited. But even this explanation does not satisfy me, since for the same reason he should have left out Saturn, which thus I have shown, he mentions. I think that here lies hidden even more deeply a mystery of the ancient wisdom of the Hebrews, among whose fundamental dogmas on the heavens, this is pertinent: that Jupiter and Mars are controlled by the Sun, and Venus and Mercury by the Moon. If we carefully study the natures of these heavenly bodies, the reasoning behind this opinion is apparent, although the Hebrews themselves offer no explanation for this doctrine.

Jupiter heats; Mars heats, so does the Sun. But, the heat of Mars is sharp and violent; that of Jupiter is beneficent. In the sun we observe the sharp violence of Mars and the beneficent quality of Jupiter; that is, as I thus said, a certain temperate and intermediate nature blended of these two. Jupiter is favorable, Mars is inauspicious—the Sun, partly good and partly bad: good in its radiation, bad in conjunction. Aries is the house of Mars, Cancer, the dignity of Jupiter; the Sun, reaching in Cancer its maximum height and in Aries its greatest power, reveals its apparent affinity with both heavenly bodies. And let us turn to the Moon, which evidently shares the waters of Mercury and which shows how great an affinity it has with Venus, especially by the fact that in Taurus, the house of Venus, it is so exalted that it is judged to be nowhere else more propitious or more beneficent. To this point, therefore, Moses has sufficiently spoken of the empyrean heaven, the ninth sphere, the firmament, the heavenly body Saturn, and the Sun and the Moon which include the rest, reminding that we include them by his very silence.

Fourth Chapter

After talking about the nature of the heavenly bodies, there remained for Moses to discuss their movements and function, declaring for what use they had been treated and for what purpose they had been assigned by God. Know, however, that up to this point the heavens have been treated simply as a luminous body and nothing has been said by the Prophet of its intelligence and of its motive force, the same sequence which the *Timaeus* also follows, first molding the body and then adding the soul to the completed body. Generally speaking, there are two manifest operations of the celestial bodies: movement and illumination. A double movement is established: one movement of the whole world by which the heavens and the air are flown around the entire space of the universe in a complete cycle in twenty-four hours; the other movement peculiar to the stars, manifold and varied, among which the principal is the movement of the Sun, which in the space of twelve months completes the circle of all the signs of the Zodiac. The former makes the day and thus is named diurnal; the latter makes the year; the other movements of the heavenly bodies are completed in various intervals of time.

Thus, directly and briefly Moses reminded us of all this when he said that the heavenly bodies were placed in the firmament for the days, the years, and the seasons. And he added "for signs," which I pass over because this has been sufficiently explained by the other interpreters.

Also, he expressly indicated the remaining operation of the heavenly bodies, which is illumination, when he said that they had been created to shine in the heavens and to light the earth. Although there are diverse opinions among the ancients as to how the celestial powers influence those below; however, the words of Moses fit any theory aptly. In fact, should their influence be only light, as Aristotle seemed to maintain, if I interpret his words not according to my own judgment but religiously, nothing is able to be conceived more in agreement with the Mosaic assertion. If, besides light, the heavenly bodies also convey heat and nothing more, as maintained by the Arabian Averrois and the Jewish Abraam, it suffices to have spoken of light, from which the same authors show that heat is also manifested. If, then, many other differnt and manifold powers are shed upon us from the heavens, as it seemed to Avicenna[8] and the Babylonians, mention of light alone was not made rashly, because, as Avicenna himself says, it is only light alone that draws to us all the remaining powers from the heavens. Therefore, the bodies of the moon, the sun, and the stars have been apportioned to these services.

Fifth Chapter

There remined for Moses to make mention of the signs which are visible in the Zodiac and of those in the crystalline sky which, although invisible to us, are, nevertheless, even more powerful. Actually, thus far, nothing has been mentioned concerning the latter; therefore, the animals which the water and the land produce represent them—especially those waters above the heavens—and the earth, which is the firmament itself, as was proved before. In fact, the constellations which are seen only in those two spheres in the shape of terrestrial animals, such as we find among us, were located by the Egyptians and the Indians, who could discover them easier and more accurately than men of our country because they were helped by the very flatness of the land and the clearness of the heavens. Otherwise, the production of the mortal animals which are here does not concern these two elements, earth and water, any more than the other two, namely, fire and air. Since Moses gave the name of water to the crystalline sphere, he fittingly called fish the animals there, and, in turn, he called pack animals and beasts those living in the firmament he named earth.

47

Sixth Chapter

So much for the corporeal nature of the heavens. Now, getting ready to declare them possessed of a rational soul, Moses remembers man allegorically, not the short-lived, terrestrial one whom we see, but the one by which, as Plotinus[9] says, the visible man is ruled. This is the same rational soul itself, which in the *Timaeus*[10] is formed of the same elements and in the same crater as the soul of the heavens, and there is not incongruously ascribed to the soul of the heavens what is said of the soul of man. The Sacred Scripture, where often every angelical and rational nature is indicated through man, agrees with my explanation. This usage is very common for the prophets with reference to the good angels and to the evil demon, who in its nature does not differ at all from them. It is written in the Gospel: ''A hostile man hath done this.''[11] Then, God added to the celestial machine a living and rational substance, partaking of intellect; and, therefore, he wished, because of its image and likeness, to rule over those animated beings I have mentioned above, namely, all the heavenly constellations and planets, which thus revolve at its nod and obey its word without any delay or obstinancy, quite differently from what happens to the immovable bodies of the elements.

You will hardly find any subject which the Peripatetics make more exertion to prove than that no heavenly body resists its mover as our bodies resist us. Thus the perpetual motion does not bring to them, as it would to us, boredom, difficulty, or fatigue. This is the divine dominion of the celestial man over the animals which Moses touches on. Similarly, it is not without mystery why God created man male and female. It is, in fact, the prerogative of the celestial souls to undertake simultaneously both the function of contemplating and dominating the bodies, and the latter cannot be an obstacle or an impediment to the former nor the former an obstacle to the latter. Especially among the ancient people, it was the custom, as we observe in the Orphic hymns, to designate by the terms ''male'' and ''female'' these two powers in the same substance, one of which contemplates while the other rules the body.[12]

These things are handed down by the Prophet concerning the

celestial world, that is, its divine body, the number of the two spheres, its nature, its qualities, and its functions. Finally, he talks about its motive power, of its rational substance, and of its intelligence.

Seventh Chapter

We should praise and proclaim this noble creation. But if we have not forgotten the Platonic doctrine, not to mention the theologians, which we recalled above saying that our souls were compounded by the divine maker in the same crater and with the same elements of the celestial souls, let us be careful not to wish ourselves slaves of those whom nature wished to be our brothers. And let us not measure our condition by this weak body.

In fact, as written in the *Alcibiades*, man is not this fragile earthbound thing we see, but a soul, an intelligence, that passes all the boundaries of the heavens and all the evolution of time. [13] Therefore, we must beware lest we contend against the will of the maker and the order of the universe, ascribing and attributing to the heavens, as many do, more than is necessary, and while seeking to please, actually displease the very heaven to whom the plans of God and the order of the world are especially at heart. The Chaldeans remind us of this, saying: "Do not magnify fate." [14] Jeremiah preaches this: "Be not dismayed at the signs of heaven which the heathens fear." [15] This our Prophet Moses prescribes elsewhere warning man to avoid admiring the sun, the moon, and the stars, lest he venerate those things which God created for the service of all the people. [16] And if someone may not accept this in the sense that the heavenly bodies must serve us as unworthy and dead bodies, we may understand what is meant is that the lords and masters of our natures cannot be substances of which parts are found even baser than are the more ignoble parts of us. In fact, in the product there neither can nor should exist anything more perfect than exists in the maker.

Let us, then, fear, love, and revere Him in Whom, as Paul says, all things have been created, visible and invisible. [17] He is the beginning in Whom God created the heaven and the earth, namely, Christ. He

Himself, having been asked Who He was, thoroughly aware of Himself replied, "I am the beginning."[18] Therefore, let us not mold in metals images of the stars but mold in our souls an image of Him, the Word of God. Let us not ask from the heavenly bodies the goods of body or fortune, which they will not give; but from the Lord of heaven, the Lord of all goods, to Whom is given all power in heaven and in earth, let us ask both present blessings, in the measure in which they are good, and the true happiness of eternal life.

THIRD EXPOSITION: OF THE ANGELIC AND INVISIBLE WORLD

Proem to the Third Book

So far, I have discussed the celestial world, unveiling the mysteries of Moses, according to the power of my ability. Now, who will give me wings, as a dove, wings plated with silver and yellow with the paleness of gold?[1] I shall fly above the celestial region to that of true repose, peace, and tranquility, in particular that peace which the visible and material world cannot give. Unveil my eyes, you spirits beyond the world, and I shall contemplate the wonders of your city, where God has laid up for those who were God-fearing those things which the eye has not seen, nor the ear heard, nor the heart pondered.

And while much about this invisible and angelic nature has been handed down by the ancient Hebrews and much also by Dionysius, it is my plan to expound the word of Moses according to the doctrine of both philosophies.

But because what is said by the Hebrews is new to the Latins, it could not be easily understood by our people unless, hatched from a twin egg, as they say, I explained a great part, or almost the totality of the ancient teachings of the Hebrew dogmas. I decided to postpone this until somewhere else I had written about Hebrew dogmas in greater detail and had made known to my contemporaries these ideas, showing how much these ideas agree with the Egyptian wisdom, how much with the Platonic philosophy, and how much with the Catholic truth. And, therefore, if I find that the Hebrews agree with us in something, I shall order them to stand by the ancient traditions of their fathers; if I find a place where they disagree; then drawn up in Catholic legions, I shall make an attack against them.

Finally, whatever I find foreign to the evangelic truth, I shall refute in keeping with my power; while any principle which is sacred and true, as from a wrongful possessor, I shall transfer from the Synagogue to us, the legitimate Israelites. Meanwhile, treading in the footsteps of Dionysius or rather those of Paul and Hierotheus, whom he followed, I shall try to bring light upon the shadows of law, which the Spirit of God, the author of law, set up for his hiding place.[2]

First Chapter

Any number, after unity, is perfected and completed by unity. Unity alone, absolutely simple, perfected by itself, does not cast out itself, but in its individual and solitary simplicity clings to itself because it is self-sufficient, in need of nothing, full of its own riches. Since number by its own nature is multiplicity, it is simple, as far as it is capable of simplicity, by virtue of its unity. And, although every number, while moving further away from unity, always falls into ever greater multiplicity with an ever-increasing variety, more parts and more composition; there is no number, however, so close to unity which would not classify as a multiplicity, having only an accidental unity and being one not by nature but by composition.

Following the Pythagorean custom, let us relate this to divine things. God alone, Who is derived from nothing and from Whom everything derives, is the most simple and indivisible essence. Whatever He has, He has from Himself. For the same reason that He exists, He knows, wishes, and is good and just. We cannot understand any reason for which He exists except that He is being Himself. Other things are not being themselves but exist by means of it.

The angel, therefore, is not unity itself; otherwise it would be God, or there would be many Gods, which cannot even be conceived. What then will be the one, if not unity itself? It follows that the angel is a number. And if it is a number, in one aspect it is a number, in another it is unified multiplicity. Every number is imperfect so far as it is a multiplicity, but perfect so far as it is a unity. Therefore, whatever is imperfect in the angel let us ascribe to the angel's multi-fold nature acquired by being a number, that is, a creature; and let us ascribe whatever is perfect to the participating unity which it shares by being related to God.

In the angel we find a double imperfection; the one consists of the fact that it is not the being itself but only an essence which shares the being by participation so that it may be; the other lies in the fact that it is not the intelligence itself but shares the intelligence and, due to its nature, has an intellect capable of understanding. Moreover, the latter, or second imperfection, is caused by the former because what does not exist by itself, certainly does not understand by itself, because there can be nothing where there is not being itself. Therefore, both imperfections exist in the angel to the extent that it is a multiplicity. It remains for its perfection and completion to happen by unity from above. God is the unity from which the angel derives being, life, and all perfection.

In the same manner that imperfection is twofold, as if a double form of the multiplicity, let us understand a double approach to unity in order that both be perfected. The first one is that by which the rough and unshaped matter exists, that is, the sterile and empty earth which God created. Nor should you believe, as others believed, that to the Creator belongs only the molding of matter and not the creation of it. Together with the earth He created the heaven, that is, the actuality of that essence and the one in the many, or the being itself; thus the creation of the heaven and the earth is almost the same thing, as it refers to things which are included in material embrace or of two natures converging, by a similar bond, toward the same end. It is not out of character with the ancient people that we call being itself "heaven," a participation of Divinity, if Xenophanes called the archetypal world a sphere[3] and both the Saracens and our own called God a "circle."

Second Chapter

An angel, from what I have said, has perfectly realized its own nature and intellectual capacity. However, it does not have a way to fulfill its powers of understanding and contemplation unless it is first adorned by God of intelligible forms. Because of this, there is darkness over the face of the deep. The deep is its intellectual capacity, penetrating and searching everything profound. Above this is darkness, until it is illuminated by the rays of the spiritual cognition with which it sees and considers everything. And it is written "over the face of the deep" and not "over the deep" because the same place is one of darkness and of light. The light, then, that is the intelligible species, covers the face, namely, the highest point of the angel's intelligence, because those qualities are accidental to it and do not pertain to its essence. The darkness having dispersed, Moses immediately adds whatever may occur before the light rises, saying, "And the Spirit of the Lord was carried over the waters."

What more will the Spirit of God be than the spirit of love? In fact, we will not, with propriety, thus call the spirit of knowledge "Spirit of the Lord" because knowledge sometimes leads away from God while love always leads closer toward God. If love is not borne upon the deep, light will not be created, because just as the eye is not filled with light unless turned toward the sun, so neither is an angel filled with spiritual light unless turned toward God. This motion of turning is not, and cannot be, anything in the angelical nature but the motion of love.

Therefore, it was the Spirit of God, the spirit of love, that was borne upon the deep, that is, over the angelic intellect (for love follows understanding), and the angel's intellect driven and excited by this love, turns toward God. "Let there be light," God said, and obviously light was made in the angel, the light of the intelligible forms; and only one day emerged from the morning and the evening because, as Averroes proves,[4] a greater unity is made from intelligence and the intellect than from matter and form, because, as the same author affirms and Moses the Egyptian writes, the truth is more easily grasped by angels than by men. And to pass over those authors, let this

54

reason be sufficient for us: the intelligible species are united to angelic minds by an indivisible bond and eternal links, instead of the unstable and temporal one as happens to human intellect.

Third Chapter

We have seen the nature of the angel created by God, that same nature turned to God in the spirit of love, finally lighted by and perfected by the light of intelligible reckonings. Now let us see in what rank angelic armies are divided. We read that the firmament was placed in the midst of the waters, by which the three hierarchies of angels are indicated to us (in fact, we shall always call them thus by the usual name). The first and the last of them are indicated by waters: the former by those above the heavens and the latter by those under the heavens; dividing them is called the firmament.

If we evaluate the natures and duties of the three hierarchies, all of these things could not be more in agreement with the doctrine of Dionysius. Since the highest hierarchy has time, as he writes,[5] for contemplation only, it is rightly represented by the waters which are placed above the heavens, that is, above all action surrounding worldly things, whether celestial or terrestrial, and they praise God unceasingly with an everlasting sound. Since the intermediate group is delegated to celestial functions, it could not be better symbolized than by the firmament, that is, the heavens. The last hierarchy, although by nature it stays above everybody and above the heavens, nevertheless, takes care of those things which are under the heavens. Because this group is divided into principalities, archangels, and angels, their influence is only on what exists below the moon. The influence of the principalities, as we learn from Daniel,[6] is around states and kings and princes; the influence of the Archangels is around the mysteries and sacred rituals. The angels take care of personal problems and each of them is assigned to men individually. Rightly, then, this subcelestial army, which presides over the mutable and short-lived things and is below the group revolving around celestial things, is represented by the subcelestial waters.

Fourth Chapter

What the gathering in one place of the waters below the heavens means would perhaps be dubious if it were not explained to us by Paul, in whose writings we read that angels sent to carry on tasks of this world are all guardian spirits sent to minister to those who receive the heritage of salvation.[7] From this we can understand that these waters below the sky, that is the angelic armies, have been congregated into one place to procure the good and salvation of man alone. From this they are sent to us and appear in different forms and places and times; after our going to sleep or even to us awake. And how this doctrine should be accepted we shall learn when we finally turn our attention to understanding how what Moses says is true: namely, that the waters were gathered together into one place. In fact, this statement is untrue if interpreted as saying that the waters cannot be found in different and distinct locations, since the Indian Ocean is divided from the Hyrcanian [the Caspian Sea], the Hyrcanian from the Adriatic, the Adriatic from the Euxine, and innumerable currents of rivers, springs, and lakes are divided by great distances. Nevertheless, it is equally said that the waters were gathered into only one location, only because these particular and divided collections of marine and river waters, all flowing towards the primary sea, as Solomon[8] says, merge and come together into the one place of the ocean. Otherwise, by no means should we understand about these angels who are taking care of the sublunar things. Different ones, in fact, preside over various corporeal and non-human affairs, because, just as the Platonists, our philosophers believed that various spiritual substances were placed by God in charge of the various corruptible things of this world. And about this Augustine resolutely asserted, as Gregory later confirmed, that nothing visible exists around us over which an angelic power does not preside, and that all bodies are constantly ruled by a rational spirit of life.[9] Similarly, Origen, in his commentaries on the book of *Numbers*, states that the world needs the angels to preside over the births of animals and also over the increase of bushes and plantings and other things.[10]

Of the same opinion was Damascene, who believed an angel that sinned was one of those of the most contemptible kind that preside over the terrestrial things. But, as all of those things below man are in reference to man, so every care, work, and zeal of the angels relative to those things is chiefly subordinate to and serves man, so that they may care for human affairs, and aiding our weakness, would let us live, as long as we ourselves allow it, piously and fruitfully.

And for this reason, Moses immediately explained what the gathering of the waters purposed: so that the earth could produce fruits, herbs, plants, and trees. What is this earth if not that one mentioned in the Gospel: some part brings forth fruit a hundred fold, some sixty, and some thirty?[11] About the earth, especially of our souls, Saint Paul writes these words: "The earth that drinketh in the rain that cometh often upon it, and bringeth forth herbs meet for them by whom it is tilled, receiveth blessing from God. But that which bringeth forth thorns and briars is reprobate, and very near unto a curse, whose end is to be burnt."[12] Accordingly, let us take care that our field will yield fruit in its own time, that it yield purgative virtues like herbs, knowledge and wisdom like larger plants, and absolute and perfect virtue like the cedars of Lebanon, so that its end may be a blessing instead of a burning. And let us hear the Father saying: "Behold, the smell of my son is as the smell of a plentiful field which the Lord has blessed."[13] Nor let anyone marvel that the heavens and earth signify one thing for me on the first day and the firmament and the aridity could mean something else now to me, which hitherto I observed in the preceding books, when both Basil and Origen and many others want heaven and earth to be one thing for Moses on the first day and the firmament and the dry earth to be something else on the second day.[14]

Fifth Chapter

Moreover, the celestial virtues help this land of ours also. In fact, the sun, the moon, and the stars were placed in the sky to illuminate the earth. See how aptly this agrees with the mysteries of Dionysius. I have spoken about the lowest hierarchy delegated to the care of sublunar things, that is, the human concerns. Now will be the explanation of the intermediate one to which is entrusted the guide of the celestial things. It should not be expected that in the same way I would speak about the third one, about which nothing can be added to what has already been said: that it is above the heavens, that is, above all motion of action, and above the administration of all worldly matter, being oriented only toward contemplation. Let us not consider this extreme or foreign to the Sacred Scriptures that Moses calls moon and sun not the heavenly bodies which we see, but the angelic virtues, the guides of the moon and the sun. Furthermore, when the Scripture says that by grace man becomes the son of God, it does not regard this mortal and fragile man whom we see, but the one who guides the man we see.

And following the Hebrew literature, in the history of kings, we read of Soloman praying in these words: "Hear me, O heaven,"[15] when he appeals, however, not to the heavens but to the lord and ruler of heaven and earth. So, it is with us in this case; when we hear of the sun and the stars, let us not think of the stars but of the angels presiding over the heavenly bodies, who, since they are invisible themselves, illuminate the earth which is also invisible, that is, the substance of our soul. It is not said either rashly or crudely that the stars were created to spread light, but said properly and harmoniously in the passages I have presented here so that my interpretation will be strongly corroborated by these if by nothing else.

Then, because (as Dionysius hands down[16]) there are three angelic functions—purification, illumination, and perfection—they are so distributed that the lowest group purifies, the highest group perfects, and the middle one, to which I am giving my attention, illuminates. The lower waters, therefore, purify our earth so that it becomes bright in appearance; the celestial waters illuminate the purified earth; the supercelestial waters perfect it with a fiery and certain vivifying dew and often fertilize it for such great felicity that there germinate not only health-giving herbs but the Savior Himself; and in us may be formed not one virtue, but Christ, the fullness of all virtues.

Sixth Chapter

Moses proceeds saying that from the elements rose a multitude of inhabitants, fishes, birds, and beasts. Here I would, indeed, be in greater difficulty than anywhere else in my work, if there did not come to my aid both Isaiah in whom we find the winged Seraphim,[17] and Ezekiel, according to whom, if we believe the Hebrews, birds and animals symbolize spiritual substances. The ancient Hebrews, all of whom, accordingly, believe that in this way Moses indicated the angelic host, hasten to assist me. Following their footsteps, let me say, then, that here the Prophet contradicted the error of the philosophers who believed (which the theologians say) that there are certain princely intellectual substances but denied that each of them presides over a great multitude as leaders preside over legions. Since, then, we have in mind nine orders of angels, and since each order has chosen by lot its own leader, let us frame that leader and prince in our minds as a great sphere and the group following him as the inhabitants and the ornament of that sphere, just as we think of the fishes in the water, the birds in the air, the beasts on the earth, and the stars in the eighth sphere. Then the word of Daniel will be true: "Ten thousand stood before him and a thousand thousands ministered unto him."[18]

Seventh Chapter

Finally, Moses mentions man, not because he is an angel, but because he is the end and the terminus of the angelic world, just as when discussing corruptible nature he did not even place man as a part of that nature but as its origin and head. From which it follows that the treatment of man pertains to three worlds: to that which is proper to him and to the two extreme ones, naturally the incorporeal and elementary, between which he is placed in the middle so that he is the end of one and the beginning of the other. But I can see a snare prepared for our interpretation, because it is also said that man is over the fishes of the sea, the birds, and the beasts. But if these symbolize the angelic nature, how can what is written be true, namely, that over them is man, whom the philosophers know and the Prophet Moses testifies is lower than the angels?[19]

Let Him Who ground Satan under our feet, Jesus Christ, the firstborn of every creature, aid us and destroy the snare. He certainly destroys the snare and unties and breaks every knot, not only because in Him, in Whom all divinity dwelt corporally, human nature is sublimated to such a level that Christ the man, so far as He is man, teaches, enlightens, and perfects the angels—if we believe Dionysius,[20] being made according to Paul better than the angels,[21] as He inherited a more splendid name—but also because all of us, to whom power is given to become the sons of God through grace whose giver is Christ, can be raised above angelic grandeur.

FOURTH EXPOSITION: NAMELY OF THE HUMAN WORLD:
OF THE NATURE OF MAN

Proem of the Book Four

Because I have shown that the Prophet sufficiently treated all the parts of the world and of all nature, celestial, angelical, and corruptible, (if I remember my promise) it remains for me to interpret again the whole reading concerning man and to prove with facts that no discussion exists in this whole work, which is concerned with the three worlds treated above, that does not thus embrace the hidden senses and the profound truths inherent to the nature of man. Nor will the effort be less worthy if, in explaining this fourth exposition, I shall remain as diligent as in the previous ones.

In fact, how useful and necessary self-knowledge is to man (to go by the Delphic saying ["Know thyself."]) was so shown by Plato in the *Alcibiades I*[1] that he left almost nothing new for posterity to contribute on this subject. And truly wicked and rash is a study of that one who, without yet knowing whether or not he can find out anything and is still ignorant himself, aims, nevertheless, boldly toward the understanding of things quite remote from himself. Then, let us come back to ourselves and see (as the Prophet says) how many blessings God created for our souls. So that for having neglected to know itself, let the soul not hear the father saying in the hymns, "If thou know not thyself, oh fairest among women, go forth and follow the steps of your flock."[2]

You see what punishment awaits us for ignorance of ourselves. In fact, we must leave our Father, and, obviously, disinheritance follows this separation. What is unhappier than this? We must also go forth completely from ourselves, for the soul that does not see itself is not in itself. Whoever goes out of himself, moreover, is rent asunder from himself. What is more painful than this? Thirdly, we must follow the steps of our flocks, that is, the steps of the beasts which are in us, of which I shall speak sufficiently in my presentation. What is more miserable than this? What more humiliating and despicable than this, namely, to become footmen of the beasts whose nature made us leaders?

Then, proceeding, not in the footsteps of the beasts but of Moses, let us enter into our very selves; let us enter, while the Prophet himself opens the way to us, into the innermost reaches of the soul to find joyously in ourselves not only all the worlds, but also our Father and our fatherland.

First Chapter

Before I arrange more accurately the words and the order of the Prophet, I must put forward some facts about the nature of man and incidentally clarify some terms, so that the sense of the whole may be more plainly understood.

Man consists of a body and of a rational soul. The rational soul is called heaven. In fact, Aristotle even calls heaven a self-moving living being, and our soul (as the Platonists affirm) is a self-moving substance.[3] Heaven is a circle and the soul is also a circle; actually, as Plotinus writes, heaven is a circle because its soul is a circle.[4] Heaven moves in a circle; the rational soul, transferring itself from causes to effects and returning again from effects to causes, is revolved by the circle of rationality. And if I explained these things separately to those who have not yet read them somewhere else, I might not be the interpreter of Moses but of Aristotle and Plato. The body is called earth because it is an earthy and heavy substance. Therefore, as Moses also writes, the name human is given to what had been made from "humus." But between the earthly body and the heavenly substance of the mind, it was necessary for an intermediary link to couple together mutually such different substances. To this function was appointed that light and airy body which doctors and philosophers call spirit, and which Aristotle writes is of diviner nature than the elements and corresponds by analogy to heaven.[5] This is called light, a name which could not fit better the theory of the philosophers and doctors who all unanimously agree that it is a particularly luminous substance and that nothing more than light pleases it, supports it, and restores it.

Furthermore, it is said that every heavenly virtue (as Avicenna writes) is conveyed to earth through the vehicle of the light, so every virtue of the soul, which I have called heaven, obviously every power, life, motion, and sense adorns and is transferred into this earthly body, which I have called earth, through the intercession by the luminous spirit.

But let us now come to the words of the Prophet. We see that first heaven and earth were created, that is, the extremes of our substance, the rational power, and the terrestial body. At the end when the light is made, that is, when the luminous spirit arrives, they are united in a way that from the evening and the morning, namely, from the nocturnal nature of the body and the morning nature of the soul, there is one man. Since every power of life and sense (as I have proved) descends to our earth through this light, justly before the birth of light, the earth was empty and void. To it heaven could not impart the benefits of life and motion except through its own intermediator light. And, therefore, the Prophet straightway placed the cause of the emptiness on the fact that before light rose darkness was still upon the earth.

Second Chapter

But as yet, the meaning of the expression "and the Spirit of God was moving on the waters" remains to be investigated. Here is stated an undistinguishable and universal doctrine of the waters, which is further specified on the following day, when Moses teaches that some waters are above the heavens and some are those below the heavens. If we want to know the true meaning of all this, let us consult nature itself which the Prophet (as often said) faithfully copies and represents.

Mention had been made of three parts of the human substance: namely, the rational part, this mortal body, and the spirit which is in the middle. Two facts still remain. Between the rational part, through which we are men, and all that is corporeal in us, whether it be gross, delicate, or spiritual, there is the intermediate, sensual part which we share with the beasts. And because sharing is no less with the angels than with the beasts, just as below reason there is sense through which we communicate with the animals, so above reason there is intelligence through which we can say with John "Our fellowship is with the angels."[6] You see what is below and what is above our reason. And if reason (as proved) is called heaven, it now becomes evident what the supercelestial and likewise the subcelestial waters in us are. The term "waters" is proper to both parts, the intellectual and the sensual, for two different reasons: the former, because it is especially transparent to the rays of divine illumination; the latter, because it stands open and is pleased by perishable and changing things. Of this difference, Moses sufficiently reminds us when he places the latter under the heavens, where are all changing and perishable things, and the former, above the heavens, where there is pure and perpetual direction of intelligence. Therefore, when we read of the Spirit of the Lord brooding over the waters on that first day and the "waters" being divided into two parts, we should not believe that it meant the waters which are below the heaven, because above these is borne not the Spirit of the Lord but rather the heavens.

It is left for a statement about those waters which are above the heavens, from whence a supreme truth about the soul is disclosed. In fact, a greater and truly divine intellect illuminates the intellect in us, whether it be God (as some like to believe) or a mind related and nearest to man as almost all the Grecians, the Arabs, and a great many of the Hebrews believe. This substance was explicitly called the Spirit of the Lord by both the Hebrew philosophers and by Abunasar Alfarabi in his book, *On the Beginnings*.[7] Moreover, it is not by chance that the spreading of the Spirit over the waters is described before Moses told of man's creation from soul and body through the bond of light. It is recalled for the following reason: lest perhaps we might not believe the Spirit to be present in our mind unless it were united to our body. Moses the Egyptian, Abubacher the Arab, and some others believed this falsely.[8]

Third Chapter

It is left that I set forth the meaning of what the Prophet calls the gathering of the waters under the heavens into only one place, that is, the sensory powers which are below the rational part. This is absolutely clear to those not altogether ignorant of philosophy. All the sensory powers flow together, as rivers in the sea, to what, for this reason, we call the common sense. (If we follow Aristotle, this is located in the heart.)[9]

Now I would not be speaking absurdly to state that from this sea the five senses of the physical body which we perceive—hearing, sight, taste, touch, and smell—diffuse, just as the five Mediterranean seas, to enter the continent of the body. This was the outspoken doctrine of Plato in the *Theaetetus*.[10] Since through the perfection of the sensitive powers, which we understand from this gathering to their own source, both life and nourishment come to that body which we call earth; immediately after the gathering of the waters, Moses justly presents the earth as green and blooming. In fact, senses have been given to all mortals by nature to look after the life and health of the body, so that through them mortals may know what is harmful and what is healthful. Then after these facts are known, through the appetite attached to the senses, they may refuse the former and desire the latter; and finally, through the related motive power, they flee the injurious and seek the useful. The eye sees food, the nostrils smell it, the feet bring one to it, the hands take it, the palate tastes it.

I am saying all this so that it will be known that with the ordering of the waters, namely, of the sensitive powers, abounding fertility is justly attached to the earth which for us by now signifies the body.

Fourth Chapter

But what has been said before, because the rational nature is distinguished by so many powers and potentialities, is only pertaining to its bare substance. Now I must tell of its ornamentation and, as I said before, its regal decoration, so to speak. This is when Moses writes that the sun, the moon, and the stars were placed in the firmament. Perhaps the more recent philosophers would, indeed, interpret the sun as being intellect in actuality and the moon in potentiality. Whereas I am engaged in a great controversy with them, let me explain, meanwhile, that wherever the soul turns toward the waters above, to the Spirit of the Lord, because it glows all over, let it be named sun; wherever it looks back upon the lower waters, that is toward the sensual potentiality, from which it contracts some stain of corruption, let it have the name of moon. In this sense the Greek Platonists might call, according to the dogmas of their doctrines, the sun "dianoia" and the moon "doxa." However, while we wander far from our fatherland and live in this night and gloom of our present life, we especially use that part of ourselves which leans toward the senses, hence we conjecture more than we know. When the day of future life has dawned, alienated from our senses and directed toward divine things, we shall understand with our superior other part. Correctly it has been said that this sun of ours presides over the day and this moon of ours over the night.

Because after casting off this mortal coil, we shall contemplate solely by the light of the sun what, in this present very miserable night of the body, we try to see with all our strength and powers more than we seem to; for this reason the day shines with the sun alone. The night, in turn, assembles and gathers for the moon, somewhat weak in power, a great many stars, as auxiliaries, that is, the power of combining and dividing, reasoning and defining, and whatever remaining powers exist.

Fifth Chapter

So much about the cognitive power of the soul. Now the Prophet turns to those whose function is to desire, that is to say, the seats of anger, wilfulness, or lust. He designates these through beasts and the irrational type of living species because we share them with the beasts and, what is even worse, often they push us toward a brutish life. From this is that saying of the Chaldeans: "The beasts of the earth inhabit your vessel," and from Plato in the *Republica* we learn that we host various species of animals,[11] so that it is not difficult to believe (if it is correctly understood) the paradox of the Pythagoreans that evil men change into beasts. In fact, the beasts are within us, right in our internal organs, so that we do not have to go very far to change into them. Hence the fables of Circe and the saying of Theocritus that those whom the goddesses, namely, virtue and wisdom, respected could not be shaken by Circe's potions.[12]

But let us see what varieties of these brutes the Mosaic writing may present to us. Some are brought forth from the waters which are under the heaven, others from the earth. The waters, as mentioned, indicate the sensual part which is under the heavens because it submits to reason and serves it more closely. The earth is this terrestial and fragile body by which we are surrounded. Let us see, therefore, whether or not some of the emotions by which we are motivated relate more to the body and others to that inward sense that philosophers call fantasy. Those which push us toward food and sexual pleasure seem to me to attend to the body. In fact, they have been given to us by God for the care of the body which we nourish, and for the procreation of offspring through which we may survive when we ourselves are dead. Enticed beyond the limit of the permissible by the urge of pleasure, we abuse these desires, through gluttony and lust, as Paul says, taking care of

67

the flesh. In his words it must be noted that he said not "Make no provision for the flesh," but "Make not provision for its concupiscences."[13] Obviously, those desires should be used for necessity, not even for pleasure; much less should our happiness be based on them. Therefore, let us consider these symbolized by animals and beasts, which are considered progeny of the earth rather than of the water because they are both satisfied and excited by limbs of this crasser body, and they have been given to us by God for its health, although they become fatal for those who exhaust themselves in excessive drinking and annihilate themselves in sexual pleasure.

However, let us relate to the waters, that is, to the sense of fantasy, those tendencies which can be considered more spiritual and to have been produced more by our thoughts than by our senses. Those tendencies which push us toward the honors, anger, revenge, and all the related feelings belong to this group. They are useful and necessary tendencies for those using them moderately. One must get angry but within limits; revenge is often a word of justice. Each one must preserve his dignity and not refuse those honors obtained by honest means. And I say this in order that, even though these animals which represent the sensual appetites are evil according to nature, we may not believe, as the Manichaeans, that they are caused by an evil origin instead of a good God having created and blessed them. All these things, therefore, are good and necessary to man, but we, being excessive in ambition, anger, rage, and pride, make evil by our sin what He the best created the best.

Sixth Chapter

Now you see how what I said fits perfectly what follows, that man was created by God in His own image to have dominion over the fishes, the birds, and beasts, which first the water and then the earth produced. Of man I talked before, but now for the first time consider in man the image of God, whence to man is command and dominion over the animals. Man, in fact, was created by nature in such a way that reason might dominate the senses and that by its law all rage and desire of passion and lust might be restrained; but, when the image of God has been forgotten through the stain of sin, miserable and unhappy, we begin to serve the beasts within us, as that Chaldean King,[14] to live among them, bending toward earth, eager for terrestrial things, oblivious of the fatherland, of the Father, the kingdom, and of the original dignity given to us as a prerogative. Evidently when man was in a state of honor, he did not understand it, but he paired himself with foolish draught-animals and became similar to them.[15]

Seventh Chapter

Indeed, as all of us—through the first Adam, who obeyed Satan more than God, and of whom [Adam] we are offspring by flesh—were dishonored and have degenerated from men to beasts; accordingly, through the newest Adam, Jesus Christ, Whose sons we are in accordance with the spirit, and Who fulfilled the will of the Father and with His blood subdued our spiritual iniquities, we have been reformed through grace and from men are regenerated in our adoption as sons of God. In us as in Him, therefore, the prince of darkness and of this world may ascertain nothing.

FIFTH EXPOSITION: OF ALL THE WORLDS IN ORDER OF SUBSEQUENT DIVISION

Proem of the Fifth Book

As I have shown in each part of his exposition, Moses dealt with all the worlds together—the intellectual, the celestial, the elemental, and the human—imitating nature, or in reality God, the creator of nature, Who in each world included all, thus imitating the example of nature which distributes to each world proper seats, proper rights, and peculiar and unique laws. Also our prophet, with marvelous and perfect mastery of the art, so composed his scripture that even though everywhere he spoke about all the worlds in the same form and with the same verbal symbols, he awarded, nevertheless, to each single world each single part of his work in subsequent order. Preparing to show this, I shall begin to interpret the first part of the first world, namely, the angelical world, then other parts of the others, wisely examining, according to Moses' words, that famous Homeric chain and the Platonic rings hanging from the living power of the creator as from the true stone of the untamed Hercules.[1]

First Chapter

About to speak of the angelic nature which is pure intellect, firstly, let us consider that the minds are like certain eyes. For what the eye is in corporeal matters, the mind is in the spiritual field. The eye, although the mixture of its own intimate substance possesses some light, nevertheless, to perform its service of vision, needs external light, by which are seen the colors and the differences of things. But this does not deny that its own nature is sight, even though it does not see without the help of light. In fact, the ears also, not to speak of the inanimate things and all the other parts of the body, are illuminated by light; nevertheless, they do not see. Therefore, the eye has received by destiny the nature of seeing and through the principle of its own essence has sight, because when it receives light, it can see.

Let us consider the same things on the intellectual basis. Intellects are eyes, the intelligible truth is light, and the intellect, being itself intelligible, has some inner light, by which it can see itself but not other things. But the intellect needs forms and ideas of things, like certain rays of invisible light, for the intelligible truth to be clearly perceived. Nor must it be said, as I have explained in the example of the eye, that the intellects are not intelligent by nature and that accidentally, like our souls, the intellectual capacity fell to our lot. From this derives the theory of those who think the intellect an unworthy title for God. Then, if we consider the intellect as the eye that cannot see for itself but only by participation of light, since God is light (in fact, light is truth), and sight is the act through which the eye receives light, God does not need this act because He is light itself, as much more remote than the angels are from any ignorance of things, just as the nature of light is farther from darkness than the nature of the eye.

But, let us go back to the angels. The eye, namely, the intellectual substance, is not all simple; otherwise, it would not endure mingling with approaching light. Hence is the common doctrine that angels consist of act and potentiality, although there is a troublesome dispute as to what the act is, what the power is, what their plan of composition is, and also what the Arab Averrois wanted to say when he stated that both intellects the active and the potential, are in all intellects short of God's; but it is enough for us, insofar as it concerns this matter, that the common opinion somehow be accepted. Moses explains to us all that I have said in the first day. In fact, he divides the angelical substance into heaven and earth, namely, the nature of the act and the nature of the potentiality.

As the same thing has different properties, so it also has different names. Therefore, as long as this same act is accepted as the virtue imparting sight to the eye and as the consummation of potency, it is called heaven, because it is, relative to the potentiality, like heaven is to earth. Again, since it is deprived of light and cannot have for itself the special gift of intelligence, it is symbolized by the waters as substance capable of receiving the light but not luminous by nature. And, there is another aspect of similarity in that this act is as close to the potency which it calls earth as water is to the earth. But, let us go back to the words of the Prophet.

God created heaven and earth, the nature of the act and the nature of the potentiality, from which He composed the angels. Indeed, earth, that is, potency, is void and empty, void of act and empty of light, which does not receive light unless through intervening waters. Since contraries refer to the same subject and it pertains to the same thing to welcome both light and darkness, he added, "And darkness was upon the face of the deep." He did not say, "upon the earth"; in fact, the deep (unless we abuse the term) is nothing more than the depth of the waters. Upon these waters was borne the Spirit of the Lord, the spirit which is called by the Apostle James,[2] "Father of the Lights," from which immediately over the waters, namely, the angelical minds, arises the light of the intelligible forms. Perhaps the Saracens understood this too when they said that "the angels were led by God out of darkness into the light and filled with eternal happiness." In fact, pleasure follows intelligence, of which nothing is greater, truer, and more lasting.

Second Chapter

Next to this world is the heavenly world, whose first property is to find itself in between two worlds, the intelligible one, which I have just described, and the sensible one in which we live. I cannot indicate more clearly the essence of any intermediate nature than by describing the extremes by which it is enclosed, since, indeed, an intermediate nature is always moderated by extremes. The Prophet then reveals to us his supreme knowledge of the nature of the heavens when he says that it is located between the waters and the waters, namely, between the angelical substances and the corruptible ones, not so much by showing their location as their essence. I have already said that by the waters are meant the forms that are closest to the potency of the earth and which perfect its essence. Just as there is one earth of angels and another earth of the elements, because the potentiality is different, so the procedure of the waters, that is, of the forms, is different for each. Between these, the heavens are truly in the middle: there, the divine life; here, the corruptible; there, the incorruptible substance; here, the visible one; there, firmness of essence; here, change of place; there, whatever is identical, simple, and uniform; here, whatever is varied, mixed, and different. In this way their lot was assigned by the distributing providence of the Maker.

Third Chapter

After these considerations on the purity, on the position, and on the order of the elements, he reminds us briefly about the gathering of the waters in only one location, also of the laws imposed upon the sea lest it flood the earth. There are in the elements, besides the tendency of a brutal and corporeal nature, laws imposed by an intelligent cause by which they are ruled and maintained within their limits. Nothing can show this better than these restraints upon the waters, by which the ocean, whose impetus might carry itself around the whole sphere of the earth in the same way that a whole sphere of fire broods over the whole sphere of air, is recalled to order as though admonished by the rod of a pedagogue, and it comes no further than our safety and the life of all living creatures demand.

All this cannot be attributed either to the necessity of the matter which had a tendency to represent spherically all elements, nor to a fortuitous agglomeration of atoms as Epicurus dreams, nor to the germinating power of the insensible nature, unaware of any end, as Strato says,[3] but only to that final cause to which only the mental and the intellectual providence can direct. Therefore, it happened that Moses, about to discuss the order of the elements, remembers this alone and that there was brought forward by the Prophets this supreme argument for the divine power and wisdom. Whence, in Proverbs is the saying that "with a certain law and compass God enclosed the depths";[4] and the other quotation that "He compassed the sea with its bounds";[5] and in Jeremiah, the Lord says, "Will not you then fear me, saith the Lord, me who have set the sand a bound for the sea";[6] and also, "Thou hast set a bound which the waters shall not pass over nor overwhelm."[7] Since the constitution of the elements is designed especially for those compound things that are alive, immediately after the fundamental ordering of the waters and of the earth, He discharged a command to earth that it germinate plants. But, on the other hand, the treatment of this work belongs somewhat to the fifth day.

Fourth Chapter

After having spoken of the celestial spheres and elementary spheres, and, therefore, of the totality of the corporeal universe, it was left to speak, as I have said, of the inhabitants and citizens of this universal city, not only of the celestial inhabitants about whom he had to speak first, almost as if of the senators and the prefects of the city, but also of the terrestrial inhabitants, as if of the plebians and the people. Therefore, he first mentions the heavenly bodies that God put in the firmament, in order that they might be for signs and seasons, to shine in the sky and to illuminate the earth: I mean the sun, the moon, and the stars. Here some very profound questions should be examined, each of which might require a whole volume. How are these stars in the firmament? Perhaps as more noble parts of it, as the Peripatetics think, or as animals in their spheres—the fishes in the waters, the cattle on the earth—as Eusebius the Mede and Diodorus prefer.

This topic would require a discussion with the astrologers, who find approval from Moses, saying that God put the stars as signs, for their knowledge of predicting through the stars and forecasting future events. Knowledge of predicting has been sharply criticized, not only by our people, as Basil,[8] who justly called it a very laborious nonsense, by Apollinarius, by Cyril, and by Diodorus, but also the good Peripatetics rejected it, Aristotle despised it, and that which is more serious, it has been repudiated by Plato and by Pythagoras and by all the Stoics, according to Theodoretus.[9] To some it may seem perhaps that here it should be investigated also about the nature, the movement, and the government of the stars, about the lunar spots and the whole knowledge of astrology. But if I condescend to these objectives, even though beautiful and worthy of knowing, perhaps I shall hear the Horatian saying, "But now was not the time for this." Therefore, I will postpone this for the projected work, in which, reconciling Aristotle to Plato, I have set out to discuss and to examine, according to my strength, the whole philosophy.

Fifth Chapter

Let us come to Moses who, after having spoken of the celestials, mentions the terrestrial animals in proper order: those who inhabit the water, the earth, or the air, if one could say that the birds inhabit the air. Let no one here expect or demand from me a discussion on how the bodies of the animals were taken from the elements and how seminal matters have been put by God in the nature of things, or whether or not the life of brutes is drawn from the bosom of matter, or whether or not all life derives rather from a divine principle, as Plotinus[10] affirms with great persistence, which soon our Marsilius

Ficinus, with public benefit, will allow us to read in the Latin language, clarified by even longer notes.

And the Prophet will seem perhaps to agree with the opinion of Plotinus in that place, where after having said, "Let the waters bring forth the creeping creature having life," he adds later, "God created every living creature." Here one might observe, however, that the waters produce, at God's command, and that God then also produces. Where the work of God is referred to, it is written: "God created every living creature"; where it deals with the waters, it is written not "living creature," but "creeping creature having life." It is as if to the water may be ascribed the vehicle of life, namely, the compounded body; but to God, may be ascribed the divine principle, the substance of the soul, which, as the origin of life, sense, and movement, comes out to give its light to the already constituted body.

But concerning this [it will be discussed] in another place. Among the animals of the earth, Moses mentions three: cows, reptiles, and wild beasts; with these divisions, there not being any more than these, he indicates to us three different species of brutes deprived of reason. The wild beasts, in fact, which are endowed with perfect senses, are assigned to a middle position among the irrational beings since they cannot be either educated nor tamed by man. The reptiles have imperfect senses and stand almost in between the animals and the plants. The cows, even though they are deprived of reason, being somehow capable of human discipline, seem thus to participate to a certain degree in reason and are allotted an intermediate position between the brutes and man.

Sixth Chapter

Until here [I have discussed] the three worlds: supercelestial, celestial, and sublunar. Now I have to discuss man, of whom it is written, "Let us make man to our image." Man is not so much a fourth world, almost a new creature, but the combination and synthesis of the three described worlds.

76

Moreover, there is a custom frequently practiced by the kings and princes of the earth, when they have founded a magnificent and noble state worthy of fame, to put in the middle of the city, when completed, their own image so that it can be seen and admired. No differently we see that God, the king of all, having built all the mechanism of the world, in the middle of it, last among the creatures, put man, created in his image and similarity. But the reason for this human privilege of man, to have the image of God, is a difficult question.

In fact, if after rejecting the foolish idea of Melito, who represented God in human form, we turn to the nature of reason and mind, which like God is intelligent, invisible, and incorporeal; on this base indisputably we shall prove that man is similar to God, especially in that part of the soul in which the image of the Trinity is represented. Nevertheless, we shall recognize that as in the angels these very traits, comparing them to us, are much more evident and without mixture, since they are more similar and linked to the divine nature.

Instead, we look at man for that characteristic which may be peculiar, in which can be found both the dignity that is proper to him and the image of the divine substance that is not common to any other creature. And what else can it be if not the human substance of man (as some Greek commentators state) which encloses within itself, because of its own nature, the substances of all the natures and the whole of the universe? I say this, because of its own essence, because not only the angels, but any intelligent creature whatever in a certain way encloses in itself all things and, when filled with all forms and reasons, he knows them.

But since God is God, not only because He understands everything, but because He unites in Himself and summarizes all the perfection of the true substance of things, so also man (even though in another way, as I will demonstrate, because otherwise God would not be the image of God, but God) gathers and connects in the fullness of his substance all the natures of the whole world.

And we cannot say this of any other creature, angelical, celestial, or sensitive. Besides, there is between God and man this difference: that God contains in Himself everything, as the principle of everything, while man contains in himself everything as a middle term of everything. From this it follows that in God all the things are of a better quality than in man himself; whereas, in man the inferior things are of nobler quality and the superior things are degenerate.

In this gross, earthly body of man, which we see, are fire, water, air and earth of the truest quality of their nature. Besides this, there is also another, a spiritual body, more divine than the elements (as Aristotle says) and which by analogy corresponds to the heavens. In man there is also the life of the plants, performing all the functions of nutrition, growth, and reproduction to him as to themselves. There is the sense of the brutes, as much internal as external; there is the soul, strong in its celestial reason; there is the participation of the angelical mind. There is a truly divine possession of all these natures flowing together simultaneously, so that we may exclaim with Mercury, "Great miracle, O Asclepius, is man!"[11]

Of this name, above all, can the human nature be proud; for this reason it happens that no created substance disdains to serve him. The earth, the elements, and the brutes are ready to serve man; for him the heavens work; for him the angelical mind provides safety and beatitude, provided what Paul writes is true that all ministering spirits are sent into the ministry for those who are destined for their inheritance of salvation.[12] Nor ought it to seem amazing to anyone for all creatures to love man, in whom they recognize something of themselves, actually their whole being and all their attributes.

Seventh Chapter

The terrestial things are needed by man; the celestial things favor him, because he is the link and tie between heaven and earth, but both cannot have peace with man unless he who in himself consecrates their peace and covenant is at peace with himself. But let us avoid, I beg, not appreciating so great an honor to be accorded. Let us keep in the mind's eye as a sure, proven, and indubitable truth that just as all things favor us, observing the law given to us; so, if through sin or collusion of the law, we depart from the beaten track, all things will be adverse, dangerous, and hostile. In fact, it is reasonable that as we do injury not only to ourselves, but also to the universe which we encompass within us, and to Almighty God, the Creator of the world itself; so also we shall experience all things which are in the world, and God especially, as most powerful punishers and most serious avengers of the offense suffered.

From here we greatly fear what punishments and torments await the transgressors of the divine law. These are the ones who, as the oracle said, wander about the land and the sea and, whenever exhausted, are vanquished by the scourge of God; these, the sky, the earth, and the whole indestructible justice of the universal city strike with lightning and pursue.

In fact, they are guilty of violating the universe and insulting the Divine Majesty, whose image they have thrust down with the filthy stain of their iniquity. For this reason, perhaps, in the books of the Prophets, when a command or a prohibition is proclaimed by God, heaven and earth are invocated as witnesses, since the transgression of the law offends them too, and as long as they serve God, they will approve the punishment of the iniquitous for the common offense. It surpasses all folly for us to believe it is right for a citizen of a state, decorated with greatest honor, to be permitted to sin with impunity against the prince and against the universal republic, which deserve the best from him, and not be delivered at once to the lictors and to the executioner to be tortured, tormented, or delivered to be stoned by the consent of the multitude of the people. In this republic of God are executioners and lictors, as evil demons, assigned to this very vile function for punishment for their sins of old. So, hence is the saying of Paul, ''I have given to Satan the destruction of the flesh.''[13]

The name of the avenging demon in Orpheus comes from this, if, by chance, we give less credit to our prophets. As every creature hates and abhors the crimes of men, thus an upright life and disposition are agreeable and pleasing to everyone. For, as I have said, all the things, being linked to man and attached with very close ties, cannot be omitted from his participation of good and evil. Concerning this is the saying in the gospel, ''If a sinner has repented, all the angels rejoice in gladness'';[14] and so manifested the meaning of that mystery hidden for centuries, that our nature, corrupted in the first Adam and dishonored by his fall, should be redeemed through the Cross of Christ.

For us the son of God became man and was nailed to the Cross. It was in harmony with all this that He, Who is the image of the invisible God, Firstborn of each creature, and by Whom the universe was created, should be joined in ineffable union to the one who was made in the image of God, who is the link of all creation, and in whom all things are confined. If, along with man, the whole nature was imperilled, his fall could not be disregarded nor could it be recovered by any except Him through Whom the whole of nature was constituted.

SIXTH EXPOSITION: OF THE RELATION OF THE WORLDS
AMONG THEMSELVES AND WITH ALL THE OTHER THINGS

Proem of the Sixth Book

God is unity so distinguished in three principles, so that He will not depart from the simplicity of unity. In each creature there are many traces of the divine Trinity. Here, I will mention only this one which to my knowledge has been presented until now by no one: the fact that the unity which we see in creatures is manifested in three forms. First of all, in things there is that unity whereby each thing is one to itself, remains the same as itself, and is in harmony with itself. There is a second unity through which a creature is united to another, and through which eventually all the parts of the world are one world. The third and the most important of all is that one through which all the universe is one with its creator, as an army with its leader. This threefold unity is present in each individual, unique thing through its own the simple unity, derived from that One, Who is the First One and the Three and One—I mean the Father, the Son, and the Holy Ghost. In fact, the power of the Father, creating everything, imparts to all His own unity; the wisdom of the Son, duly placing everything, in

81

turn unites them and links them together. And the love of the Spirit, directing everything to God, joins the entire work to the creator with a bond of love.

In that manner, as God is closer to us so He is more one than we are with ourselves; in turn, each thing is united with itself more firmly than with the other parts of the world. Therefore, taught the order of universal love, if we wish to follow the Divine Law written on the tablets of nature, first, we shall love God Himself above ourselves and above all, second, we shall love ourselves, and third, our neighbor.

Our Prophet spoke enough about that unity by which each thing is one to itself when he examined singly the nature of things. The unity for which we are linked to God will be treated in the next exposition, where I shall discuss the supreme felicity. There is left the one unity for which all the different parts are united among themselves with a mutual bond, and of this [unity] I must speak now.

Chapter First

Since I have considered the distinct nature of things, as I have said, and placed them in separate places, we must not believe that one universe was made from all of these, due only to this mutual rapport that each individual thing has with the other, according to the nature of its condition. The Prophet in his text also wanted to show how many and what were the manners through which the different natures of things might be united among themselves, not only stimulating us toward a careful understanding, but teaching and showing us through which way and plan we can be united with what is more useful for us. And while I was pondering, before starting the reading of the words there were or could be considered through which things might find an affinity or a reciprocal bond, and while enumerating all the doctrines of the philosophers on which I have sweated from boyhood, I could not recall more than fifteen types. After reading from Moses, I saw underlined so distinctly and suitably by him these types that I believe nowhere else can any one be better taught about them.

Second Chapter

Immediately, on the first day, I do not know whether more concisely or more clearly he deals with the five ways in which two things can be united with one another. In fact, what is united with something else either is its essence, or is the property of its essence, or is contained in it as a form by a subject, or affects it either by changing what is changed or as an art affects the matter subject to it. Similarly, we read from Moses of five things compared as if united: the heavens and the earth, the earth and the void, the deep and the darkness, the Spirit of God and the waters, the light and the bodies. Therefore, the void and empty earth represent the first kind of unity for us, because the earth, meaning the matter, is by its nature void unless it is filled with forms from outside.

The second kind of union is shown by the darkness on the surface of the abyss, because the deep is by its nature neither luminous nor obscure, but the nature of the deep is darkness if a coming light does not chase it away, as the shapeless and emptiness of matter receives the darkness of deprivation until the coming form drives it out.

The light rising from the bodies shows the third light. In fact, light is to them as form is to the subject.

The fourth is shown by the heavens and the earth, since the heavens are not connected to earth as a form or an accident is contained in the thing which it is perfecting but are united to it as active cause to passive, or as a cause of change to the body which is changed. Of this last type of union, an example is the Spirit of God which moves over the waters. In fact, the creative wisdom of God and the spiritual nature completely disattached from the matter of the body are understood as united to the bodies only as art—which is in the mind of the architect —is united with mortar, wood, and stones.

Also consider this plan of natural succession, that earth in itself is empty in its native darkness, and then it is joined to the light and through the light to heaven, and through heaven to the spiritual substance. But let us see just how things are arrayed in us. The earth is the terrestial body without life, insensible, and upon it are darkness, death, numbness, impotence, immobility, insensitivity. The light is life which enlivens, excites, stirs, and moves the body, and provides it with sense. Heaven is the soul, the source of that light; and the Spirit of God is the intellect, the light of the divine countenance. This is more than is necessary about these matters in this place.

Third Chapter

Let us examine what Moses wants to say in the following verses, and we shall see that insinuated by him are ten other ways [of unities], in which we may understand the mutual bond of certain things. In fact, besides those already mentioned, there are also these which I shall enumerate: one thing is either a part or result of another; if it is a part, either it is a part indivisible from the whole, as are the sun the moon, and the stars in the firmament, or separable, as the parts of water are from the wholeness of their element toward which they flow together. If it is an effect, either it springs from an inner seminal reason, as plants spring from the earth, even though still attached to the mother, and linked to her by ties and natural links; or it is made up and composed of its materials as a mixture from the elements, as the bodies of the animals are made of water and earth; or it has an extrinsic cause that can be divided in three forms: efficient cause, model, and end. We have examples of these three from Moses, when God creates man, when He completes the creation and makes man according to His own image, as a model, and when beasts are under man and are created for man, as for an end.

Fourth Chapter

We have spoken of the part and of the effect, and at the same time of the whole and of the cause. In fact, these discussions correspond to each other. But we have not completed all the kinds of relationships. Of cause there remains that kind of affinity for which the secondary

84

cause obeys and is united to a primary one, in the same manner as when God produces, the waters produce, not only as the causes closer to Him, but without departing from God's direction, since primary cause influences more than secondary.

In the same way, a secondary end exists, depending on and connected to the principal one, which Moses wisely indicates by saying that the stars were placed to shine in the heavens and illuminate the earth. In fact, the welfare of the inferior things is not the primary end of the celestial bodies. They intend first to shine for themselves, then finally, to shine for us. Therefore, also in Homer we read that the dawn and the sun rise and bring light first for the immortals, then for the mortals. Besides all these relationships, man is linked to man, and lion to lion, even though the lion is neither a part nor an effect of a lion unless he has been born of a lion. The Prophet shows this when he collects and puts together the fishes, the birds, and the animals of the earth. There is a last kind of affinity: that which exists between the nature of a mean and the extremes. In fact, man is close to man, the animal, to the animal, because they share the same kind of essence whether of species or of gender. But the mean is not of the same essence as the extremes, but somehow compounded from them; it differs from both of them so that it may communicate with both. Moses indicated this to us when he puts the firmament in the midst of the waters, dividing the waters above the heavens from the waters below the heavens, where he sufficiently clarifies the nature of the mean, as I declared at length in the proem of the first book and in the second chapter of the fifth book.

Fifth Chapter

Let us be reminded from this what we must do to be united to better natures, on which depends the whole and highest force of our felicity. In fact, the first day teaches us that the light, after night was chased away, first arose over the waters when the Spirit of the Lord brooded over them. Whence the saying of James is explained: "that every perfect gift comes from above, from the Father of the lights."[1] Not to mention our Christians, Jamblicus[2] confirms this when he states that the human nature cannot do anything, or at least can do only mediocre things, if it is not helped by a superior nature, that is, the divinity. If this is true and supported not only by our fellow thinkers but also by the philosophers, certainly all our zeal ought to be turned to higher things to seek strength for our weakness through holy religion, the mysteries, vows, hymns, prayers, and supplications. Therefore, the Platonic and Pythagorean disputes are born and are terminated with the sacred prayers, than which nothing is more useful or more necessary to man, according to what Porphyry and Theodorus and all the other Academicians unanimously affirm. The Indian Brahmans and the Persian Magi are quoted as never doing anything unless a prayer has been said. I bring in these testimonies of the pagans so that those who have been persuaded by an evil spirit to believe them rather than the Church may learn even from those on whom they bestow their faith that it is neither ridiculous nor useless nor unworthy of a philosopher to dedicate himself assiduously to sacred prayers, mysteries, vows, and hymns jointly sung to God. If this is worthy and most becoming to the human race, it is particularly useful and beautiful for those who have devoted themselves to the study of letters and the life of contemplation. For them nothing is more necessary than to purify with integrity of life those eyes of the mind which they turn toward the divine, again and again, and to illuminate them with the light from above through the use of prayer and, mindful of their own weakness, they may say with the apostle, "Our sufficiency is from God."[3]

Sixth Chapter

Let us now examine again what the distribution of the water and of the earth teaches us.

From the earth let us learn that we will not produce the crop we generated unless we restrain and drive back the deluge of the flowing and perishable material attacking us and push away from our bodies the whirlpools and torrents of pleasure rushing upon us like water.

From the waters let us learn that they were not thought suitable for procreating the fishes until they were collected into a total unity of their whole element.

In fact, if we have been distracted and turned aside to a variety of things, and if when all energies have been gathered, we are not carried forward toward one end, neither shall we be able to create an offspring worthy of our divinity. In the distribution of the waters is also hidden this even deeper mystery: just as it is plainly the final happiness of drops of water to reach the ocean, where there is the fullness of the waters, so our happiness consists in being able one day to join that spark of intellectual light that is in us with the first intellect of all and the first mind, which is the fullness and the totality of all understanding.

Seventh Chapter

But above everything, the doctrine of the firmament signifies for us that the lower waters cannot be enriched by any gift from the upper ones except by intervention from the heavens, which is located between them, so let us understand that the union of the extremes cannot be effectuated except through that nature which, as a mean between them embracing both, unites them easily since it has already united them through the propriety of its own nature.

Let us be led back to the great sacrament that is madness to heathens, a scandal to the Hebrews, and the virtue and wisdom of God for us: that man can be united with God only through Him Who—since in Himself He united man to God—can, as a true Mediator, so unite men to God that just as in Him the Son of God put on manhood, so through Him men are made sons of God. And if it is true what we have said: that the extremes can be united only through the mean; and if that rightly is called a mean which in itself has already reunited the extremes; and if that ineffable grace by which the Word becomes flesh can be realized only in Christ, then it is only through Christ that the flesh can ascend to the Word; and there is not (as John[4] correctly wrote so well) under the heavens another name through which it is possible for men to be saved. Let them deligently consider this, who, even when they say that they believe in Christ, however, believe for each man that the common religion, or that one in which each one was born, may be enough for gaining felicity. Let them not believe either me nor the reasons themselves, but John, Paul, and Christ Himself, Who said, ''I am the way; I am the door; whosoever does not enter through me is a thief and a bandit.''[5]

SEVENTH EXPOSITION: OF THE HAPPINESS WHICH IS THE ETERNAL LIFE

Proem to the Seventh Book

If, with the completion of the sixth exposition, I have exhausted as in the six days, the degrees, the order, and the nature of the world, in this seventh treatise, almost the Sabbath of my commentary, it remains for me to tell of the Sabbath of the world, and of the repose, that is, the felicity of the creatures we talked before, namely, of their felicity or happiness; to speak more correctly, it is left to hear Moses spinning it out as a true prophet of all the future things.

There is, as the theologians state, one happiness that we can reach through nature; the other we can reach through grace. They call the former the natural one and the latter the supernatural. Of the first, the natural one, enough has already been said by Moses, and since their nature is known, we know also their natural happiness.

It is left to him, therefore, to tell about the second, rather exhibiting himself as a prophet than as a teacher, since when Moses wrote, grace did not yet exist, but it was going to exist in the future.

But because I seem to see certain scholars, or better said, some idlers and good-for-nothings who, calling themselves philosophers while they are not, regularly laughing at both grace and supernatural happiness as if they were empty names and old wives' tales, I have wanted to have a brief discussion with them about this fact, just as a proem to the seventh book—a thing in itself useful to everyone and very necessary to the work that I have assumed, where I prove that the opinion of the theologians is strongly based and established on the deepest roots of philosophy.

I define happiness thus: the return of each thing to its own beginning. Happiness, in fact, is the supreme good; the supreme good is that which all seek; that which all seek is the beginning of everything, as Alexander of Aphrodisias, in his commentaries of the first philosophy,[1] and the Greek interpreters of Aristotle's *Ethics* confirm. The end and the beginning of all things are the same; they are the one God, omnipotent, blessed, best of all the things that can exist, or can be thought of; hence are those two names among the Pythagoreans, the One and the Good. He is called One because He is the beginning of all, as unity is the beginning of every number, and Good because He is the end, the rest, and the absolute felicity of all things. By now, if we are a little more perceptive, we can discern the principle of this double beatitude. Happiness, in fact, is the possession and the attainment of the first goodness. The created things can achieve it in two ways: within themselves, or in Him. In fact, in itself this good is exalted above all, inhabiting the depths of its own divinity; in all things it is found diffused, here more perfectly, there less so, according to the condition of the things with which it is shared.

Therefore, as the poets write, Jupiter is wherever you look, and all the things are full of Jupiter.[2] Every nature, therefore, has in itself God in some degree because it has as much of God as of the good (all the things that God created are good). It remains that when it has perfected its own nature in all respects and has attained its potential that it may also attain God within itself; and if the attainment of God, as we have demonstrated, is happiness, in some manner it is happy in itself. This is the natural happiness that greater or smaller the various things have allotted according to the diversity of their natures. The fire is a thing lacking a soul, but it participates in God in many respects. In fact, first it exists, and everything which is exists by participation in God, Who is Being Itself; besides, as far as fire is a definite species and action, it is similar to God, Who is the First Species, the First Action. Finally, when fire creates fire, it imitates within the limits of its nature, the divine fertility; when it constrains itself within the boundaries of its sphere, it imitates justice; when it serves us, it imitates benevolence.

When fire does these things, it has attained its perfection and is as happy as it is capable of happiness; happier are the plants that also have life; even happier are the animals, which have been allotted consciousness, so that the greater perfection they have, moreover, the more divinity they find within themselves. In a condition superior to that of all mortals is man, who, as in nature, in natural happiness exceeds all the others, gifted with intelligence, free will, and special qualities very conducive to felicity.

Supreme among the creatures is the angelic mind due to nobility of subtance and the obtainment of its goal, in which it especially participates because it is close and united to it. But, as I said before, through this happiness neither plants, nor animals, nor men, nor angels reach God—Who is sublime good—within God Himself, but within their ownselves. Due to this fact and the capacity of nature, the degree of happiness varies gradually. Therefore, the philosophers having spoken only about this put the happiness of each thing in the best operation of its own nature. And even concerning the angels, whom they call minds and perceptions, and whose supreme perfection they acknowledge because the angels know God, nevertheless, they did not acknowledge any other cognition of God besides that one with which they know themselves, so that the angels understand only as much about God as the nature of God is represented in their substance. Concerning man, even though different philosophers give diverse opinions, nevertheless, all have kept within the limits of the human capacity, limiting the happiness of man either by the investigation of truth, as the Academicians do, or by its attainment through the studies of philosophy, as Alfarabi said.

Averois, Avicenna, Abu Bakr, Alexander, and the Platonics seem to concede something more, founding our reason, as on its exclusive end, on intellect, which is on impulse [or on] something higher, nevertheless [known to us;] but these lead man neither to his beginning nor his end. I do not reproach nor despise these arguments and sentiments, provided they seem to speak only about natural happiness. But it is certain that, through this [natural happiness], neither man nor angels can be exalted higher than what they say.

And this is proved especially by the fact that, if nothing can rise above itself by relying on its own strength (otherwise it would be stronger than itself), in the same fashion, nothing relying on itself can rise to any greater or more perfect happiness than its own nature. But let those philosophers tell me why, if in the order of things there exists only this happiness, they themselves recognize that, among the animals, only man was born for happiness. In fact, although other things besides man also reach their ends, we can say that their happiness is inferior to man's; but in which way shall we defend this? Moreover, since the inferior beings never come out of the limitations imposed by nature, while man almost always goes beyond them, his condition, unless it claims some other privilege, seems the least happy of all. Let us listen to the sacred theologians reminding us of the dignity of our nature and of the divine goods very freely offered by the very generous Father, I pray, lest cruel in our own souls and ungrateful toward God the Creator, we reject them. We have said before that the supreme happiness is in the attainment of God, Supreme Goodness, and the Beginning of everything; furthermore, that this attainment can happen in two ways, since we reach God either in the creatures in which He participates or in God Himself. Also I have shown, and I will come back to the subject, that created things cannot reach with their strength this ultimate happiness, but only the former one. And that one, if we think it over, is more a shadow of happiness than real happiness, as the creature in which you attain God is not the supreme goodness, but a pallid shadow of the supreme, that is, the divine goodness.

Add the fact that, through the former happiness, things are restored to themselves rather than to God, with the result that they do not return to their own beginning but simply do not become separated from themselves. While the true and complete happiness brings us to the contemplation of the countenance of God, that is, the absolute Goodness, as He Himself said, and to the perfect union with that beginning from which we emanated. To this happiness the angels can be raised, but they cannot ascend to it. Therefore, Lucifer sinned, saying, "I will ascend into heaven."[3] To this happiness man cannot go; he can only be drawn; therefore, Christ, Who is the Felicity Itself said of Himself: "No man comes to Me unless My Father has drawn him."[4] Animals and things inferior to man can neither go nor be drawn to that happiness. Therefore, only men and angels are created for that happiness which is the true happiness. The vapor can go up, but only attracted by the rays of the sun; stone and all material substances can neither receive rays in any way nor be lifted up by them. These rays, this divine force, this influx, we call grace because it makes man and angel pleasing to God.

The philosophers have a clear example of this doctrine in bodies. In fact, some bodies are borne in a straight line and others are borne circularly. The straight movement, by which the elements are borne to their proper locations, represents that happiness through which things are established in the perfection of their own nature. The circular movement, through which a body is brought back to the same place from where it came, is the most express image of the true felicity, through which a creature returns to the beginning from which it sprang.

But see how everything comes together on both sides. Only the immortal and incorruptible bodies move in circles. No substance returns to God unless it is immortal and eternal. The elements, to complete their motion, need no other force than the impetus ingrained in them of gravity and levity, as single things are attracted to natural happiness by their own proper impetus and force. But the heavenly bodies, even if suitable for circular movement, are not sufficient by themselves to accomplish this motion but have need for the divine motor to turn and move them around. Finally, those bodies are thus adapted to the eternal circular movement, not in the capacity of producing it, but in the capacity of receiving it. It happens not at all differently for the angels and for us.

Our nature is such that we cannot turn around in a circle and turn back upon ourselves, but we can be turned around in a circle and brought back to God by the motive power of grace. Hence comes the saying. "Whosoever are led by the Spirit of God, they are the sons of God."[5] "Who are led," it says, not "who lead." We differ from the heavens which are moved by the necessity of their nature, while we are moved according to our freedom. In fact, the moving spirit pushes assiduously against your soul. If you fail to hear, you will be left miserable and unhappy to your torpor and your weakness. If you admit it, you are carried back at once, full of God, through the orbit of religion to the Father, to the Lord, to possess eternal life in Him, in Whom you always had life even before you were born. This is the true happiness: to be one spirit with God, so that we possess God, not by ourselves, but by Himself, knowing Him as we are known. For He knew us not through ourselves, but through Himself. Thus, we shall know Him through Himself, instead of through ourselves. This is our whole reward, this is eternal life, this is the wisdom which the wise men of this world have ignored: that we are brought back from all the imperfections of the manifold to unity through the inseparable link with Him Who is Unity Itself.

For this happiness Christ prayed to his Father in this manner, "Father, bring it about that just as you and I are one, they also may become one in us."[6] This happiness Paul hoped for, saying, "I shall know Him, not in part, but as He is."[7] And if he hoped so, did he not say rightly, "Who will separate me from the love of Christ?"[8] And he desired to be dissolved to become one with Christ. From this happiness fell the devil, because he wanted to climb up to it, not to be lifted to it, and so he lost what he would have had if he had remained in this condition. On this basis is known the destiny of infants who die not yet baptised. They remain as they were, not stripped of their goods nor enriched by divine ones.

We must fall into one of the two ways, either supreme misery or supreme happiness. Because he who does not receive the moving spirit not only makes himself immune to grace but also violates his own nature, [whose] integrity requires him to seek the known spirit and not refuse it; and without a doubt, the nature which rejects or despises the hope of a greater possible good cannot be right. Therefore, after having known Christ, whoever are not arrayed in Christ are deprived not only of the first happiness, but also of the second one, namely, the natural happiness, because not wanting the grace is typical only of a corrupted and fallen nature.

As we, living under the gospel, receive Christ in ourselves, as the power and wisdom of God, because we love Him as already given to the human race, and we draw close to him, so also the Fathers under the ancient law received Him, because they believed in His future coming and eagerly hoped for it and ardently desired it. But just as

94

they accepted Him not as already present but as yet to come, they did not enjoy in the present the fruit of the Indwelling Spirit until after the Christ had come. Then after the ineffable sacrifice was carried out on the altar of the cross and Christ's coming down to them, by Him, as by a motive force, they were caught up to freedom with the moving power of a tornado and lifted up to the position of supreme happiness; so we use philosophy as a conductor for the natural happiness. But if nature is a rudiment of grace, then philosophy is a rudiment of religion, and a philosophy does not exist that separates man from religion.

Therefore, after having philosophized for six days about nature, going back to Moses, I on approximately the seventh day, at leisure for divine things, shall speak of the supernatural happiness.

First Chapter

As I have shown, the nature capable of this supreme happiness can be twofold, both angelic and human. The former is called the heavens, the latter is called earth, because the angels live in the heavens and we live on earth. Moses does not say any more about the heavens, since he is not going to write the law of the angels, but of men. Coming down to men, then, he says, "The earth was void and empty, and darkness was upon the face of the deep." God does not create a void, and He does not create darkness, but, as the Prophet says, the earth was void and there was darkness. He does not say that these were created, but that they were.

Why he said this will be evident when we know what this void and darkness are. Compared to the angels, human nature, which is called earth, immediately from the beginning, because it sinned at the beginning, was void and empty of its original justice; and its surface, namely, reason, was covered by the darkness of sin. God did not do this, but the malice of man, who willingly deprived himself of those gifts with which God enriched him. So the state of the corrupted nature is described by the Prophet, and in what follows he will demonstrate how it was restored to its pristine dignity and prepared for the supreme happiness by Abraham, by Moses, by the prophets, and ultimately by the only begotten Son of God. But, also when the waters were covered by darkness, namely, corrupted by the primal stain of the original sin, the Spirit of God brooded over them. And this has to be understood in two ways: first, that men were guided by the light of the divine countenance that is stamped upon us, namely, by the light of the natural intelligence; and second, that at this time the human race was not deprived of the care of the Divine Providence. The Spirit of the Lord brooded over the waters, that Spirit which (as the Apostle says) interceded for us with indescribable groanings,[9] and it was continuously considering by what means it might purify the waters from the poison with which the ancient snake had corrupted them; when behold, He commands the light to rise, and the light rose.

The very wise Abraham was the first founder of the true religion, the first one to unbind himself from the natural law of nature and to meditate upon the divine law, the first one to persuade men to the cult of one God alone against the idols of the Gentiles, the first one who began to disperse the darkness of error and to make war on the evil demons who are called the princes of darkness, whence, light is correctly synonymous. Since all the disciples of the Lord did this also, all have been called by the Lord "the light of the world." This is the first light which shone on the world and that distinguished between the worship of demons and of the true God, somewhat like the difference between light and darkness.

Second Chapter

The law followed this, which deservedly is called "firmament," announcing to us at once in its very proem, that is, in this very part which I am now treating, the work of the hands of God, as David sang, "and the firmament declareth the work of His hands."[10]

Thereupon, the law given through the angel to Moses was confirmed by the Work of God which, hitherto, more than the greater light, distinguished other people from the Israelites, namely, impiety from piety, as supercelestial waters from the waters that are below the heavens.

The Jews are called supercelestial waters because only they, as Jeremiah says,[11] do not fear the signs of the heavens, which the other people fear; only they do not fear the stars nor the heavens, but recognize the Creator and Master of the stars and the heavens, and they worship and adore Him, Whom they recognized. For the opposite reason, the Gentiles are the waters under the heavens, since they adore and worship the demon inhabitants of the misty air, which is the region above the waters, and make the visible heavens, stars, and planets their gods and lords.

Third Chapter

Unless some greater strength and mercy of God had blocked the way, the waters that are under the sky, I mean, the servants of the idols, would have invaded and occupied the whole world.

Thus, the corruption of the whole world from the first stain demanded this; and the command and law of the vindictive Satan over us demanded it, guilty as we are of the ancient sin and liable for the punishment of such a servitude. But the ever beneficent and salutary providence of God wanted one part of the earth, but only as small as the laws of His justice allowed, to be free from the injury of the waters. This is Judea, called the land of promise, which was promised by God to Abraham and posterity.

All the prophets agree with my interpretation, and by them the frequent attacks of other people on the Israelites are compared to the floods of the waters of the sea. Whence are these sayings: "The floods have lifted up their voices,"[12] and "wonderful are the surges of the sea,"[13] and "their waters roared and were troubled,"[14] and "we will not fear when the earth shall be troubled and the mountains shall be moved into the heart of the sea."[15] In fact, the Gentiles surrounded Judea, enclosed within the boundaries of a region, not at all large, as now on all sides the ocean surrounds this modest portion of earth that

97

we inhabit. But in many places in the Christian scripture the Gentiles are indicated very obviously as the waters. In fact, it is written, "The waters which you have seen are Gentiles,"[16] and when Jesus our Lord made wine from the water because it was lacking in the house of the Pharisee, he signified, as our prophets write, that the waters, namely, the Gentiles, were to be called to that faith which in the future would be lacking to the Jews, among whom earlier it had existed. Likewise, in the mysteries are handed down the fact that water is mixed with wine because the waters of the Gentiles drink and absorb the blood of Christ through the faith of the cross.

That part, then, was delivered from the yoke of the waters by the providence of God so that, if the rest of the earth should be submerged by the waves of spiritual iniquity and should become useless, deserted, and not suitable for the fruits of true religion, at least there would be this part. Having received the light which the first day brought forth and fertilized with the dew of the heavens which were made on the second day, namely, by the doctrine of the law, this part would then germinate judgments, ceremonies, and good customs, just as herbs, plants, and trees, until, when the fullness of time had come, it would also germinate with supreme happiness the very Saviour, Whom Isaiah beseeched.

Fourth Chapter

And lo the fullness of time! For if the number four is the fullness of numbers, in the world of numbers, will the fourth day not be the fullness of days?

See then what the fourth day brings us. On the second day the heavens were created, namely, the law, without sun and moon and stars, certainly capable of future light, but for the moment still dark and not illuminated by any remarkable light.

Then came the fourth day on which the sun, lord of the firmament, namely, Christ—Lord of the laws, and the lunar Church, Christ's consort and wife, similar to the moon, and the apostolic doctors, who would educate many to justice, as stars in the firmament—began to shine for eternity, calling the world to eternal life. The sun did not destroy the firmament, but fulfilled it, and Christ came not to destroy the law, but to fulfill it.

The light of the first day, namely, the very pious Abraham, saw the fourth day, which is the day of Christ, and rejoiced. He saw that the rays of His light, that is, of the true religion which He had brought into the world by the sun of justice, were to diffuse very widely in the whole universe through the true light illuminating all men. He saw Jesus Christ, the splendor of the Fatherly Substance, shining upon these who were entrenched in darkness and in the shadow of death, and he saw that the prince of darkness, the prince of this world, was cast out and banished from the minds of men. He saw these things and exulted; he saw the fourth day and was glad, this day which the Lord made, in which the Lord became man, and in which God dwelt among us. Let us also exult in it this day and let us be glad.

Oh Christian brothers, I pray that you consider a little more diligently how true and sound is my exposition, whence to you there will be furnished, against the stony hearts of the Hebrews, very powerful darts taken from their armaments. I shall prove then, first that from the testimony of the Jews, through the work of the fourth day, is shown to us the coming of Christ. Secondly, I shall show that the Messiah is represented to us by no symbol better than the sun; and by a calculation of time, I shall deduce with absolute evidence that Christ will not come in the future, but that Jesus of Nazareth, the son of the Virgin, was the Messiah promised to the Hebrews.

Among the decrees of ancient Hebrew wisdom is the fact that through the six days of the Genesis are symbolized the six thousand years of the world, so that what are here called the works of the first day were a prophecy of what was going to be in the first millennium of the world, likewise, the works of the second day, of what was going to be in the second millennium, and so on, with always the same order of succession on either side. Among the more modern thinkers, Moses of Gerona, a theologian of great renown among the Hebrews, proves this doctrine. Saint Jerome also mentions it in the exposition of that Psalm which is assigned to Moses,[17] and this opinion seems to have the firmest support in the principle that a thousand years, as the Prophet says, are one day before God.

The fourth day, then, if this doctrine is true, is the prophecy of what is going to happen in the fourth millennium of the world. Now let me show that, according to the annals of the Hebrews and the calculation of those years which they approve, that Jesus appeared in the fourth millennium of the world. They count 1556 years from Adam to the flood, 292 years from the flood to Abraham, and so from Adam to Abraham are computed 1818 years. From the birth of Isaac to the ruin of the second temple, which was after the death of Christ, they compute around 1660. From Isaac to the exodus from Egypt they compute 430 years; and from the exodus to the temple that Solomon built, they compute more or less as many years; from Solomon to the destruction of the temple by the Babylonians, 410 years; from the building of the temple under Ezra to its capture under Titus, 420 years.

So, if you add all together, from the origins of the world to Christ you will count, according to the reflection of the Hebrews, 3508 years, so that Christ came in the very middle of the fourth millennium. Within the limits of the same millennium, as within the limits of the fourth day, the light of the moon, namely the Church, shone over the whole world, and the innumerable multitude of martyrs, apostles, and doctors who all became renown within 500 years after the death of Christ illuminated the darkness of our night and the obscurity of the firmament, that is, of the law.

Yet the Hebrews will say, "Granted that Jesus came at this time, but you have not proven that Jesus was the Christ, unless you show that it was believed by our people that Christ would come at that time." It is a good point, and they ask it fairly, and I can easily prove what they rightly request. In fact, among them, the oracles of Elijah are spread as commonly understood traditions, which say openly, and without any symbolism or veil, that the Messiah will come in the fourth millennium of the world.

Lest these facts seem feigned or arbitrarily interpreted by me, I shall cite the testimony of the Talmudists themselves, with whom I am in controversy. They not only mention these oracles but, with the very truth forcing them, confess that the time for the advent of the Messiah predicted by Elijah has passed. These words are in the part entitled *Aboda Zara*,[18] under the heading "libne edeem." So let me, translating word for word in Latin, interpret this: "Sons or disciples of Elijah said: the world has six thousand years: 2000 for the creation, 2000 for the law, 2000 for the day of the Messiah, and on account of our sins, that are many, there have passed those which have passed.'' So they say. Come now, with these very words placed before the eyes of all, I cannot introduce any comment too free or even arbitrary. Let us break up and examine the words of the oracle and be at once masters of the proposition. The world, says the Prophet, has six thousand years, which we may interpret either in this way that after the lap of six thousand years, as many of our people have also believed, the end of the world will come, just as the Sabbath; or if (which is more exact) no one knows that day, we may interpret it in the sense that nothing in the law is held as prophecy of time further on. However, this does not pertain to the proposed question. Let us see what follows: 2000 years, the vacuum; 2000 years, the law; and then, the Messiah.

The Prophet calls the vacuum as all the Hebrew commentaries say, the time before God handed down any law to men. But I see a Jew leaping upon this and saying, "If 2000 years are before the law and 2000 years for the law, then the Messiah was going to come not on the fourth day, namely, while the fourth millennium was finishing, but rather on the fifth day, that is, after the fourth millennium." But the response is easy, since undaunted truth provides it. What was said by Elijah—2000, the vacuum, 2000, the law—must not be interpreted as if the world, for the whole period of 2000 years would be without law, and, similarly, that for 2000 years would the law remain, but interpreted in the sense that the time of natural law will last up to the second millennium and the time of the law will last up to the fourth one.

But before the second is finished, the law will come, and before the fourth one has elapsed, the Messiah will come. I neither make up nor dream this interpretation for myself. The very Elijah teaches me this, and the very Talmudists teach it too. This also to you, Jewish viper, unless you might plug your ears, will soon be manifest. Elijah says, "2000 years, the void and 2000 years, the law." Let us see in what sense that which is said about the void was true, and from that let us learn how to explain what is said of the law. We take the beginning of the law either from Moses or from Abraham. It cannot be taken from Moses because the void would then have lasted more than 2300 years or about that. It is almost that long from Adam to Moses.

101

Therefore, the beginning of the law must be taken from Abraham, to whom the covenant was given of circumcision, the root and foundation of the whole ancient law. If then the Jews consult their stories, they find that from Adam to Abraham there has not transpired an entire period of 2000 years, but only of 1848. From which it comes about that not after the second millennium, but within its limits, the fullness of the law followed the void. And for the same reason, the fullness of the gospel had to follow the void of the law, not after the fourth millennium, but while the fourth millennium was going on. And if they proceed to deny this impudently and even insistently, let them hear their own Talmudist strongly supporting my version. In fact, at the time when they were writing, they confess that the time for the advent of the Messiah, predicted by Elijah, had passed, and they ascribe this to their own sins. If the words of Elijah were interpreted in the sense that Christ would come after the fourth millennium, and not within the limits of the fourth, the Talmudists neither would not have nor could have said that the time of the Messiah promised by the prophets had passed. Moreover, when the Talmudic doctrine was written, as I have reported, not yet 4000 years after the origin of the world had passed. For as I have shown above, Jesus appeared 3508 years after the origin of the world, according to the Hebrews. The Jerusalem Talmud, however, (as they themselves account) was written 300 years after the death of Christ, and the Babylonian 100 years after the Jerusalem Talmud. Therefore, each was written within the limits of the fourth millennium and, nevertheless, both acknowledge and complain that the time predicted by Elijah for the coming of Christ has passed.

Now where will they hide themselves, or what hiding places will they seek to flee completely and not see at all our sun, to their vexation, illuminating the whole universe? The Talmudists confess, even if they do not believe the ancients, that the times predicted by the prophets for the coming of Christ have gone past. They confess that according to the prophets it was believed Jesus would come during that time, during which they themselves consider that Jesus came. And their doctors are not completely untruthful when they affirm that the Messiah did not come because of their sins. In fact, He did not come for those who did not acknowledge Him. He is not the Messiah, that is, the Redeemer of the worst captivity, the beneficent King, the Rewarder of the promised land, that is, of the heavenly Jerusalem, save only for those who recognized Him as the Messiah.

Moreover, if His people did not receive Him coming to earth, they are no more His who were His; but from the East and from the West come those who rest in the bosom of Abraham, while the chosen people are thrown out into the outer darkness. Whence is solved the grievous inquiry about the fact that the Messiah would have been for the salvation of the Jews, while Christ has been for their ruin. In fact, they are not Hebrews, who do not follow and worship the King and Lord, promised to the Hebrews from the house of David, but who instead fasten Him to the cross as a thief, as a profane person, and a blasphemer with every injury and insult. If they were sons of Abraham, they would remain unmoved in the precepts of Abraham and would receive joyfully the coming of this day, the fourth, in which Abraham took pleasure in forecasting it.

The Messiah has brought peace to men, but not to all. In fact, by the angels it was not simply said, "and on earth peace to men," but there was added, "to men of good will."[19] Certainly the same sun which gives light to pure eyes, blinds and darkens the weak and sick. And by a just plan it happens that He Who is salvation for the good ones is noxious for the evil ones; and He, Who, powerful and beloved, blesses His friends, likewise hurls lightning and disperses enemies. If evil had come to the Jews after Christ had been accepted, he would not have been Christ. But if evil came to them for having crucified Him, then He was certainly Christ, Who, even when nailed to the cross and He appeared completely defeated, triumphed over His conquerors with so much destruction and calamity for them.

Why then do you blind ones wait for the sun? The sun is here and shines, but it shines in darkness and your darkness[20] does not comprehend it. The fourth day has passed when the sun rose which has not destroyed the law but fulfilled it, as the sun does not destroy the firmament, but adorns, fulfills, and illuminates it. I have proved from the order of the fourth day and the time of the advent of Christ that what is said here must be understood as referring to Him. Let me prove the same thing through similarity by a figure of speech, because through no other way can we better imagine Christ than through the sun. In fact, He put his tabernacle in the sun and went out from the tribe of Judah, whose symbol is the lion, the solar animal; and if Plato in the *Republic* calls the sun the visible son of God, why may we not interpret it as the image of the invisible Son?[21] If He is the true light, illuminating all mentality, does He not have as a very express likeness the sun, which is the sensitive light illuminating all bodies? But what else do we look for? Let us interrogate the very sun, which, eclipsed behind the moon during the passion of Christ, manifestly showed us the unanimity of its nature.

So rightly, not to touch on a higher reason, the day which the astrologers call the day of the sun, we have called the Lord's day, and we have consecrated it wholly to His cult. Hence, we have shown that there is no further purpose for us to venerate (as once did the Gentiles) the physical sun as king and lord of the heavens, inasmuch as, the invisible sun, co-eternal and co-equal to the Father, by Whom both the heavens and earth were made, has illuminated men sitting in the shadow of death.

Fifth Chapter

But let us examine now whether or not the works which follow the fourth day correspond to what is ascertained to have happened after the advent of Christ, in order to accept my exposition finally as true and fixed when we have learned that everything agrees and re-echoes with it. Let us see what happens after the fourth day. The waters produce the fishes and the birds; the land produces cattle and beasts of burden. Let us call to mind what I have said before was symbolized by the waters, which, located under the heavens, were gathered into one place; and likewise, what I have said was symbolized by the earth which was made immune from their overflowing. I have said that by the waters are symbolized the Gentiles, by the earth, the Israelites, and I have confirmed this not only with many testimonies of the prophets but also by principles of similarity.

We have also seen that before the rise of the sun, the sterile waters produced nothing which was good; the earth, indeed, was producing, but producing only poor fruits, small cabbages, and herbs. After the arrival of the sun, the waters, with productivity greater than that of land, produce two kinds of animals: birds and fishes. The land, no more satisfied with trees and fruit plants, produces a great many of cattle and beasts of burden. Do you not see, even with me silent, the completed prophecy of the good Simeon, that our sun might be a light to the revelation of the Gentiles and to the glory of your people, oh Israel?[22]

Do we not have it before our eyes, if we interpret nothing otherwise, both the calling of the Gentiles and the transformation of the earthly Jerusalem and of the shady synagogue into a true church and the eternal and celestial city of God? The waters produce nothing before the rising of the sun. The earth produces something, but meagre and poor. Because before the coming of Christ there was among the Gentiles no sign of life, no fruit of the true religion. Among the Israelites there was indeed some hope, and they knew in part the path of light and revered the true religion, but imperfect and primitive, until He came Who is the path, the truth, and the life.

And unless we return to this mystery, let someone give me the reason why He divided the ornaments and progeny of the earth, so that He produced some before the sun and others after the sun. Moreover, why do waters produce nothing before [the arriving of] the sun, while the earth produces something? Why are two kinds of living animals produced from the waters and only one from the earth? Why is the bird, the animal of the air, assigned to the waters? In fact, (to speak about the first one) it is not enough to say, as some have said, that the herbs and the plants were produced from the earth before the creation of the sun lest they might seem created by its power. For even more, by the same principle, the fishes, the birds, and all the perfection of the elements should have been created before the sun, lest their making be believed by its [solar] power.

Moses then would have left a suspicion that, even though it might not have been necessary for the light of the sun to produce imperfect things, like plants; however, it was necessary to produce animals, which are more perfect. Following logically, if the more perfect things might come into light without its helping, the less perfect could also have been made without it. However, the plan cannot be reversed so that if the ignoble things, like plants, the lowest kind of living things, had been made without it, all kinds of animal natures could also have been produced without the intervening of its work.

Therefore, the plan of the Prophet is discovered more truly from what I have said. Similarly, if anyone says that to the waters have been assigned the animals which live in the waters, he will see rather that only one kind of animal ought to have been assigned to the waters, and two kinds to the land, because land more than water is the home of the birds. And if, beyond all controversy, we consider the nature of the animal, the bird is an animal of land or air, in no manner aquatic.

But hear the most profound reasons of all, even against our wills, attracting us to the mysteries of Christ and the Church. And certainly if all things, as Aristotle says, agree with the truth, all things must agree with Christ, Who is the very truth. Not without reason, nor for nothing, did he say so often to the Hebrews, "Search the Scriptures; the same are they that give testimony of me."[23] And He asserted that many things, indeed all things, were predicted of Him in the Laws, in the Psalms, and in the books of the Prophets. But often we are blind in front of so much light; only by his unveiling our eyes are we able to consider the wonders of his law. With him bearing the work for us, let us come to the revelation of the mysteries and the symbols. From the waters two kinds of animals are produced, one from the land because there was a greater number of believers among the Gentiles than among the Jews. However, the land produces more perfect animals than those which the waters produce, even though much less numerous, namely, the beasts of burden and all the quadrupeds. Even though more of the Gentiles than of the Hebrews believed; nevertheless, the more perfect believers were Hebrews, from whom came the Apostlic founders of the whole religion. Similarly, the waters produced different species and a two-fold nature, that of fishes and of birds, but the land produced only one nature, since among the Gentiles some are converted to Christ from the service of demons, others from the law of nature.

Every Hebrew is a Hebrew only because to him it is not permitted to live within the limits of nature, and to whom the law of God was given as peculiar and not common to the other people. In fact, God did not behave the same with all the nations and did not manifest to them His judgments. The fishes, therefore, indicate those who came to us from the demons' cult, not only because the waters, as I showed before, symbolize the impiety of the Gentiles, but because Jonathan the Chaldean proves that evil spirits are often portrayed in the Sacred Scriptures by the animals that live in the waters.

The birds symbolize those who from the laws of nature are brought to grace, and the reason for this is clear from what I wrote at length in the proem of this book about the natural and supernatural happiness. I showed, in fact, that the heavens were the most express semblance of supernatural happiness, and that natural happiness was rather something secondary and imaginary than true happiness. Therefore, those who follow this using the laws of nature are very suitably denoted by the birds, inhabitants not of the first and true heavens, but of the air, which also takes for itself the name of the heavens for a secondary and imaginary reason. Therefore, in the Sacred Scriptures, they are often called winged creatures of the heavens and birds of the heavens.

See with what deep wisdom the birds are assigned not to air but to water. Those who lived according to nature were also considered Gentiles, who obviously called themselves Gentiles, and lived among the Gentiles, as Socrates perhaps and the majority of the philosophers. For this reason both species have been jointly assigned to the waters. But how much this exposition agrees with the evangelic doctrine, how much with the apostolic doctrine is at hand to demonstrate. Indeed, the Apostles, converted from the Hebrews, have been symbolized by Paul in the oxen,[24] terrestrial animals, and, moreover, by our doctors of the Gospel, pictured in that location where the merchants are driven out of the temple,[25] and where Christ calls the Israelites sheep.

The Apostles, then, to whom the conversion of the people was committed, have been called fishermen by the Lord, and of them the prince is Peter, who was to be a fisherman at Rome, Mistress City of the Gentiles, like a fisherman[26] of whales in the ocean.

Christ, Who said that He was not sent except to the lost sheep from the House of Israel, took for Himself not the name of fisherman, but of shepherd.

Sixth Chapter

Hence is also clear the solution to the question which for so long has tormented the interpreters of Genesis: why on the second day did Moses not say, "And God saw that it was good"? It will not seem fully satisfactory if I say what is accustomed to be said, that this was not done because the work of the waters was not finished on that day, but on the third one, on which the waters that are under the heavens flowed together into one place. In fact, the particular work of that day is not the arrangement of the waters, but rather the arrangement of the firmament, which was secured in the midst of the waters. On that day was perfected the creation of the firmament when God said, "Let there be a firmament made," and the variation of the waters when God said, "And let it divide the waters from the waters." Enough finished.

And as the gathering of the waters, which is called the sea, and the uncovering of the earth, and the production of the plants have an arrangement of an altogether different work, so they were completed on another day, that is, the third, to which they belonged. Moreover, the explanation of a deeper mystery must be investigated. The firmament, as I have shown before, represents the law. And the firmament was unformed and simply imperfect until it was furnished with the sun, the moon, and the stars, just as the law was not, in fact, bad (as the Manicheans said) but simply not good—I mean perfect, until Christ came, Who fulfilled the law. If the firmament had been bad, it would not have received the sun; if it had been good, it would not have needed the sun.

But the firmament was good so far as it was capable of receiving the sun and the other stars, just as the law was good so far as it was a teacher for us about Christ; and because of the insensibility of his people, Moses permitted many things which later the Gospel did not permit. Moreover, we cannot call the law bad, as Manes believed; neither can we call it good, as the Prophet very openly teaches. According to Moses, God speaking of the Jews says, "I gave them statutes that were not good."[27] He did not say "bad laws," but "not good laws," namely, not perfect, not completed, not final [laws]. The ancient Hebrew doctors confirm this. Interpreting this passage of

108

Ecclesiastics, "Vanity of vanities, and all is vanity,"[28] they say that even the law is vain until the Messiah should come.

And so much indeed about this.

Seventh Chapter

Moreover, the supreme favor of the incarnate Word was that, through the sacrament of Baptism through which is transfused into us the virtue of Christ, we may be reborn as sons of God, born not of blood, but of God. At the end Moses shows us this when, after the sun has risen and been shown to the world, and after the fertilization of the waters and the land, God makes man in His own image, not the earthly man, but the heavenly one. When the Gentiles and the Jews had been converted to Christ, it was left for them, making themselves according to the cross of the Lord, to be remade in the image of God. For if baptism makes men sons of God, and the son is the image of the father, is not the virtue of the whole trinity operating in Baptism given in these words, "Let us make man in our image"? If then we are in the image of God, we are also in the [image] of the Son. If we are sons and heirs, we are heirs of God, co-heirs of Christ. But who are the sons? It is written by Paul that we shout aloud "Abba" (Father) in the Holy Spirit.[29] Consequently, those who live in the Spirit are sons of God, brothers of Christ, predestined for the eternal inheritance, which they will happily take possession of in the heavenly Jerusalem as the reward for their faith and life well lived.

EXPOSITION OF THE FIRST EXPRESSION, NAMELY, "IN THE BEGINNING"

Now has come the end of the work with the exposition of the whole text having been surveyed in its seven forms. However, I recognize that as yet there has been something left by me untouched and undiscussed which it seemed should have been explained even at the first, namely, what the first expression of the law means, that is, "In the beginning."

Moreover, neither casually nor without reason, have I wanted to speak of this beginning at the end of the whole work. I am neither going to discuss here the son of God, Who is the Beginning through which all the things have been created (for He is the wisdom of the Father); nor am I going to prove in this place that the ancient Hebrews believed the same; I shall do that somewhere else. But I plan to give my readers a taste of the Mosaic profundity through another method of interpreting.

I shall not do this before I have gathered a few facts on a certain dogma, which is really a paradox of the ancient Mosaic teaching. It is a firm decision of all the ancients, a fact which they affirm as with one voice, without doubt, that in the five books of the Mosaic law is included the entire knowledge of all arts, and of all wisdom, both human and divine, but disguised and hidden, however, in the same letters from which the expressions of the law have been composed— by what method now I shall disclose.

Let us take, for instance, the first part of the Book of Genesis, I mean, from the beginning up to the place where it is written, "And God saw the light, that it was good." This whole scripture has been composed of 103 letters, which placed in the manner in which they are there, make up the words that we have read, offering nothing through itself but the common and trivial. Obviously the orders of the letters, this text, forms only the bark of a secret kernel of hidden mysteries. But if, after the words are taken apart, we take separately the same letters, and, according to the rules which Hebrews hand down, we join them together correctly into expressions that can be made with them; they say that, if we are capable of hidden wisdom, very wise and marvelous dogmas about many things will shine out to us. If this is done with the whole law, then finally, there will be brought to light, by both the correct position and connection of elements, every doctrine and the secrets of all the liberal disciplines. I state this, however, if we are capable of occult wisdom. Certainly it can be that to us, drawing and taking apart and uniting some expressions, may be born many words, and likewise a manifold chain of oratory which may teach and signify deep meaning. However, unless someone has followed the learning of that matter elsewhere, not knowing what those ideas signify, he can disdain them as useless and accidental.

Thereupon, we cannot learn, but only recognize dogmas and doctrines. I do not prove nor attest to these things because I have not made an experiment of them nor do I believe I can do it. However, I neither deny nor condemn this opinion, not only because this has many supporters, but also because from Moses, who was trustworthy concerning the whole house of the Lord, even greater revelations may be easily believed. I thought, therefore, that it would not be displeasing to men of my time, if I made public these gems, superior to those, in the opinion of the poets, either the Hermus and Pactobus are said to bear, which showed themselves to me while skirting the shore without even entering its depths.

I should like to explain the first expression of the work, which by the Hebrews is read "Bereshit" and by us "In the beginning," to see if I also, using the rules of the ancients, could draw out into the light thence something worthy to know. And beyond my hope, beyond my conjecture, I found what not even I, finding it, could believe, nor what others could easily believe—the whole arrangement of the creation of the world and of all things revealed and explained in that one expression.

I do say a marvelous, unheard of, and unbelievable thing. But if you will pay attention, you will believe it at once, and the very thing will prove me right. That expression by the Hebrews is written in this manner: בראשית, that is, Berescith. From this if we unite the third letter to the first, it becomes אב, that is, "AB." If to the first one doubled, we add the second one, it becomes בבר, that is, "BEBAR". If we read all of them except the first, it becomes ראשית, that is, "RESIT." If we unite the fourth and the first and the last, it becomes שבת, that is, "SCIABAT." If we put the first three in the order in which they are, it becomes ברא, that is, "BARA." If with the first omitted, we put down the three following ones, it becomes ראש, that is, "ROSC." If leaving out the first and the second ones, we put the two following ones, we have אש, that is, "ES." If we leave off the first three ones, we put together the fourth and the last one, we have שת, that is, "SETH." Again if we unite the second to the first one, we have רב, that is, "RAB"; if we put after the third, the fourth and then the fifth ones, we have איש, that is, "HISC"; if we unite the first two with the last two, we have ברית, that is, "REBITH." If we unite the last to the first, we obtain the twelfth and the last word, תב, that is, "THOB," turning the THAU into the letter THETH, which is a very common proceeding in Hebrew.

Let us see what these words mean in Latin, then what may be revealed about the mystery of the whole nature to those not ignorant of philosophy. AB means the father; BEBAR means in the son and through the son (in fact, the prefix BETH means both); RESIT indicates the beginning; SABATH the rest and the end; BARA, created; ROSC, head; ES fire; SETH, foundation; RAB, of the great; HISC, of the man; BERIT, with an agreement; THOB, with goodness.

If, following this order, we rebuild the expression, it will be like this: "The Father, in the Son and through the Son, the beginning and end, or rest, created the head, the fire, and the foundation of the great man with a good agreement." This entire discourse results from the taking apart and the putting together of that first expression. It cannot

112

be clear to all how deep and full of all meaning this teaching is. But, if not all, at least some of the ideas are signified to us by these words that are clear to all. By all Christians it is known what is meant by the saying "the Father created in the Son and through the Son," and likewise what is meant by "the Son is the beginning and the end of all things." In fact, He is the Alpha and Omega, (as John writes),[1] and He called Himself the Beginning, and we have shown that He is the End of all things in which they may be brought back to their beginning.

The rest is a little more obscure: namely, what do the head, the fire, and the foundation of the great man mean, and what is the "agreement," and why is it called "good"? In fact, not everyone can see present here every law of the four worlds of which I spoke, the whole plan, their relationship, and, likewise, their happiness, about which I explained at the end. First then, we must remember that the world was called by Moses, "great man." In fact, if man is a small world, necessarily the world is a great man. Hence with the opportunity seized, he pictures, very appropriately, the three worlds, the intellectual, the heavenly, and the corruptible ones, through the three parts of man, not only showing with this figure that in man are contained all the worlds, but also explaining briefly which part of man corresponds to each world.

Let us consider then the three parts of man: the higher is the head; then that which from the neck stretches to the navel; the third, that which extends from the navel to the feet. And these parts in the figure of man are also well defined and separated with a certain variety. But it is astonishing how beautifully and how perfectly they correspond by a very precise plan, by analogy, to the three parts of the world.

The brain, source of knowledge, is in the head; the heart, source of movement, life, and heat, is in the chest; the genital organs, the beginning of reproduction, are located in the lowest part. By the same token, in the world the highest part, which is the angelic or intellectual world, is the source of knowledge because such nature is made for the understanding; the middle part, that is the sky, is the beginning of life, of movement, heat, and is controlled by the sun as the heart in the chest. It is known to all that below the moon is the beginning of creation and corruption. See how appropriately all these parts of the world and of man correspond reciprocally. Indeed, he designated the first one with its appropriate name, the head; he called the second one fire, because by this name the heavens are valued by many, and because in us this part is the principle of heat. He called the third one foundation because by it (as is known by all) is founded and sustained the whole body of man. He added finally that God created them with a good agreement because between them, through the law of divine wisdom, an agreement of peace and friendship was decreed on the kinship and on the mutual agreement of their natures. This agreement is good because it is thus arranged and set in order toward God, Who is goodness itself, so that, just as the whole world is one in the totality of its parts, so also like this, at the end, it is one with its Maker.

Let us also imitate the holy agreement of the world, so that we may be one together in mutual love, and that simultaneously through the true love of God, we may all happily ascend as one with Him.

NOTES

NOTE TO ROBERTO SALVIATI GREETS LORENZO DEI MEDICI

[1] Dedication to Lorenzo dei Medici by Roberto Salviati, the publisher in 1489 of the original edition.

NOTE TO HEPTAPLUS OF GIOVANNI PICO DELLA MIRANDOLA

[1] The Septuagint.
[2] *Acts* 7:22.
[3] Numenius, a 2nd century Syrian Neoplatonist, a forerunner of Plotinus, Fr. 13 (Thedinga).
[4] Eusebius, *Praeparatis Evangelico* X.1,4; Clement, Stromata I.15.66
[5] Porphyry, *Vita Pythag.* 57 (ed. Nauck, p. 49); Jamblic, *Vita Pyth.*, XXVIII, 146; Philostrati, *Vita Sp. Th.*, I, 2 sgg.
[6] Porphyry, *Vita Plotini*, III, 24 sgg. (ed. Brehier, p. 3).
[7] Plato, *Epistle* II, 312 d-e.
[8] *Psalms* 119:11.
[9] *Ezekiel* 8:2.
[10] *John* 1:1
[11] *I Corinthians* 5:11.
[12] Pseudo-Dionysius, *Caelestis Hierarchia* II (Migne, *Patrologia Graeca*, III, 133 ff.)
[13] St. Jerome, *Epistle* LIII (Migne, *Patrologia Latina*, XXII, 547).
[14] *Deuteronomy* 24:19.
[15] *Matthew* 9:37.

NOTE TO SECOND FORWORD OF THE WHOLE WORK

[1] Plato, *Phaedrus* 247c.
[2] Simplicius, *Physica* 27.2.

[3]*Psalms* 136:5.
[4]*Hebrews* 1:7.
[5]*Ezekiel* 1:16 ff.
[6]*Mark* 16:15.
[7]*Exodus* 25:40.
[8]*Romans* 14:3.
[9]Augustine, *De Genesi ad litteram* V,3 (6) (Migne, P. L., XXXIV,323).
[10]Propertius, *Eleg.* III, 1, V. 6.
[11]J. Pomerius, *De vita contemplativa*, I, prol., 2 (P. L. LIX, 415 b).

NOTE TO MOSES' WORDS TO BE EXPOUNDED

[1]*Genesis*, 1:1-27.

NOTES TO THE FIRST EXPOSITION

[1]Averroes, *De Substantia Orbis* I.
[2]Aristotle, *Metaphysics* XII, 2, 1069; *Physics* I, 6, 189a.
[3]M. Terentius Varro, *De Lingua Latina*, V, 59 (Goetz and Schoell).
[4]S. Thom. Aquinas, *Summa Theologica*, I, q. LXVI, a. 2.
[5]Aristotle, *Physics* I, 7, 191a; Plato, *Timaeus*, 52b; cf. Zohar I, 16a ff.
[6]Albertus Magnus, *Summa Theologiae*, II, tr. 1, q. 4, m.2 (*Opera*, XXXIII, 90ab); I, tr. 3, q. 15, m.2 (Opera XXX, 100a).
[7]Aristotle, *Physics* I, 6, 189a.
[8]Aristotle, *Posterior Analytics* II, 13, 96b.
[9]Ecclesiastes 1:4.
[10]Alexander of Aphrodisias, 2nd century commentator on Aristotle.
[11]Heraclitus, fr. 31. Proclus, *Theologia Platonica* VI,22.
[12]Ennius, *Achilles*; cf. Nonius Marcellus, ed. Lindsay, I, 248.
[13]Aristotle, *De Plantis*, A 1, 815a.
[14]of Plato and Aristotle.
[15]Plato, *Timaeus* 39c; 40d.

NOTES TO THE SECOND EXPOSITION

[1]Dionysius Areop., *Caelestis Hierarchia* VII; Aquinas, *Summa Theologica*, I,q. 89, a.l.
[2]W. Strabo, *Glossa Ordinaria in Genesim*, I,1 (Migne, P.L., CXIII, 68c); Bede, *In Pentateuch* (Migne, P.L. XCI, 192).
[3]Ezekiel 1:26.
[4]Zachariah 4:2-3.

5Emperor Julian, *Opera*, ed. Hertlein, I, 171-175.
6Aristotle, fr. 204, Rose.
7St. Augustine, *De Genesi ad Litt.*, I, 18(36). (Migne, P.L. XXXIV, 260); cf.
Basil, *Homilia II in Hexaemeron*.
8Avicenna, *De Caelo et Mundo*, 14. Cf Aquinas, II *Sententiarum*, d. 13, q.
1 a.3.
9Plotinus, *Enneads* I, 1, 10.
10Plato, *Timaeus* 41d.
11Matthew 13:28.
12Damascius, *De Principiis* 123 (Ruelle, I, 317).
13Plato, *Alcibiades* I, 124 ab.
14*Oracula Chaldaica*, ed. Kroll, p. 50.
15Jeremiah 10:2.
16Deuteronomy 17:3.
17Colossians 1:16.
18John 8:25.

NOTES TO THE THIRD EXPOSITION

1Psalms 55:6.
2Psalms 18:11.
3Aristotle, *De Melisso Xenophane et Gorgia*, 3, 977 b.
4Averroes, *De Animae Beatitudine* (ed. Giunta, 1573, IX, 153 ab).
5Pseudo-Dionysius, *Caelestis Hierarchia*, VII ff.
6Daniel 7.
7Hebrews 1:14.
8Ecclesiastes 1:7.
9Augustine, *De Diversis Quaestiones* LXXXIII, I, 79 (Migne, P.L. XL, 90).
Cf. St. Gregory, *In Ezeckiel*, I, 7.
10Origen, *In Hieremias* VIII (Migne, Patrologia Graeca, XIII, 364-365).
11Matthew 13:8.
12Hebrews 6:8.
13Genesis 27:27.
14Basil, *Hexaemeron* III, 3 (Migne, P.G., XXIX, 56-60; Origen, *In Genesim*,
I, 1-2 (Migne, P.G., XII, 145-148).
15Kings 8:32.
16Pseudo-Dionysius, *Caelestis Hierarchia* XI.
17Isaiah 6:2.
18Daniel 7:10.
19Psalms 8:5.
20Pseudo Dionysius, *Caelestis Hierarchia* IV.
21Hebrews 1:4.

NOTES TO THE FOURTH EXPOSITION

[1]Plato, *Alcibiades* I, 124a ff.

[2]*Canticle of Canticles* 1:7 (Song of Solomon 1:8)

[3]Aristotle, *De Caedo*, II, 6, 289; Plato, *Phaedrus* 245c.

[4]Plotinus, *Enneads* IV. 4, 45.

[5]Aristotle, *De Spiritu* I, 481.

[6]I John 1:3.

[7]Cfr. Alpharabii, *De Intellectu et Intellecto*, ed. Gibson (*Archives D'histoire Doctrinale* et *Litteraire au Moyen Age*, 1929, p. 126), 392-99.

[8]*Ibn Baja, Epistola Expeditionis*, in Munk, *Melanges de Philosophie Juive et Arabe* (Paris, 1927), pp. 393 ff. [Moses the Egyptian, 1135-1204].

[9]Aristotle, *De Anima* III, 2, 425 b.

[10]Plato, *Theaetetus* 156 a.

[11]Plato, *Republic* 588d. Cf; Eusebius, *Praeparatio Evangelica* XII. 46.

[12]Theocritus, *Idyllia* IX, 33-36.

[13]Romans 13:14.

[14]Daniel 4:30.

[15]Psalms 49:12.

NOTES TO THE FIFTH EXPOSITION

[1]Homer, *The Iliad* VIII. 19-20; Plato, *Theaetetus* 153 c-d; Eunapius, *Vita Sophist*. (Boiss, p. 7); Marinus, *Vita Procli*, 26; Damascius, acc. Photinus, cod. 242.

[2]James 1:17.

[3]Cicero, *Academica* II, 121; *De Natura Deorum* I, 35.

[4]Proverbs 8:27.

[5]*Ibid.*, 29.

[6]Jeremiah 5:22.

[7]Psalms 104:9.

[8]Basil, Hexaemeron, VI, 5-7 (Migne, P. G., XXIX, 128 ff.); cf. Eusebius, *Praeparatio Evangelica* VI, 11 (Migne, P. G., XXI, 477a-480a).

[9]Theodoretus, *De Providentia* 5 (Migne, P. G., LXXXI, 624).

[10]Plotinus, *Enneads* VI; VII,8.

[11]*Asclepius* I.6 (*Hermetico*, ed. W. Scott, I, 294).

[12]Hebrews 1:14.

[13]I Corinthians 5:5.

[14]Luke 15:10.

NOTES TO THE SIXTH EXPOSITION

[1]James 1:17.
[2]Jamblichus, *De Mysteriis Aegyptiorum* II. 11; V, L4. Porphyry, *Ad Marcellam*, 18; St. Augustine, *De Civitate Dei* X.9.
[3]II Corinthians 3:5.
[4]John 20:31.
[5]John 14:6.

NOTES TO THE SEVENTH EXPOSITION

[1]Alexander of Aphrodisias, *In Metaphysician Commentaria*, ed. Hayduck, p. 820, lines 25 ff.
[2]Vergil, Eclogue II. 60. cf. Augustine, *De Civitate Dei IV*, 9-10 (P.L., XLI, 119); Albertus Magnus, *Commentaria de Causis*, lib. I, t. IV, c. V; *Summa de Creaturis*, II, q. V, a.2.
[3]Isaiah 14:13.
[4]John 6:44.
[5]Romans 8:14.
[6]John 17:21.
[7]I Corinthians 13:12.
[8]Romans 8:35.
[9]Romans 8:26.
[10]Psalms 19:1.
[11]Jeremiah 10:2.
[12]Psalms 93:3.
[13]Psalms 93:4.
[14]Psalms 46:3.
[15]Psalms 46:2.
[16]Revelations 17:15.
[17]Psalm 90.
[18]*Aboda Zara*, 9a; cfr. *Sanhedrin*, 97a; *Zohar*, I, 25a.
[19]Luke 2:14.
[20]John 1:5.
[21]Plato, *Republic*, VI, 508e.
[22]Luke 2:32.
[23]John 5:39.
[24]I Corinthians 9:1-12.
[25]John 2:14.
[26]Matthew 4:19.
[27]Ezekiel 20:25.
[28]Ecclesiastes 1:2.
[29]Romans 8:15; Galatians 4:6.

NOTES TO THE EXPOSITION OF THE FIRST EXPRESSION

[1]Revelations 1:8

GLOSSARY OF PROPER NAMES

Aba or Abba Aricha (c. 175-247 A.D.): Jewish teacher in Babylonia.

Aboda Zara: reference about the coming of Christ found in the Zohar, a medieval mystical work on the Pentateuch and the definitive work of Jewish Cabala.

Abraham ben Meir ibn Ezra (1092-1167): "Abraam the Jew"; commentator and interpreter of the Pentateuch.

Abubacher, the Arab: 12th century Moorish philosopher and physician.

Aegidius Romanus (c. 1247-1316): theologian and philosopher of Scholasticism; teaching based chiefly upon the authority of the church fathers and of Aristotle and his commentators.

Albertus Magnus (c. 1193-1280): "Albert the Great"; German Scholastic philosopher; teacher of Saint Thomas Aquinas.

Alexander of Aphrodisias: 2nd-century commentator on Aristotle and teacher in the Lyceum at Athens.

Alfarabi or Mohammed Abu-Nasr al-Farabi (c. 870-950): Arabic philosopher from Aleppo and Baghdad.

Ambrose, Saint (c. 340-397 A.D.): bishop of Milan and teacher of St. Augustine.

Anaxagoras: 5th-century B.C. Greek philosopher; held the doctrine that matter was set in motion and ordered by intelligence.

Anchelos: 1st-century translator into Greek of the Targum, an Aramaic interpretation of the Pentateuch.

Apollinarius the Younger (c. 310-390): Syrian Bishop and propounder of the idea that the Logos replaced the rational human soul in the nature of Christ.

Aquinas, St. Thomas (1225-1274): the "Common Doctor" of the Church, whose work in systematizing Christian Doctrine according to Aristotelian philosophy dominated the thought of the Middle Ages.

Aristotle (384-322 B.C.): Athenean philosopher and former student of Plato; founder of the Lyceum or the Peripatetic School; works were much translated by the Arabian scholars during the Middle Ages.

Augustine, Saint (345-430 A.D.): one of the Latin fathers in the early Christian church.

Averroes (c. 1126-1198): Arabian philosopher and physician in Spain; his interpretations of Aristotle were regarded by some as heretical; he taught a pantheistic doctrine of Universal Reason and denied the immortality of the soul.

Avicenna (980-1037): Arabian physician and philosopher; commentator on Aristotle and Galen.

Basil (Saint "Basil the Great"): 4th century A.D. bishop of Caesarea.

Bede ("the Venerable Bede," c. 673-735 A.D.): English monk, historian, and theologian.

Cabala (also Cabbala, Kabala, Kabbala): System of esoteric theosophy developed by rabbis from about the 7th to the 18th centuries, reaching its peak during the 12th and 13th centuries; based on a mystical method of interpreting the scriptures to penetrate sacred mysteries and foretell the future.

Caesar Julian (331-363 A.D.): "The Apostate"; Roman emperor, 361-363 A.D.

Chaldean: ancient Semitic people of Babylonia; pertaining to astrology; Jewish writers in Arabic.

Chrysostom, St. John (c. 347-407): Patriarch of Constantinople.

Cicero, Marcus T. (106-43 B.C.): Roman statesman, orator, and Stoic philosopher.

Cyril, Saint (376-444 A.D.): archbishop of Alexandria.

Damascene: St. John of Damascus; 8th century philosopher.

Democritus (c. 460-361 B.C.): called "the laughing Greek philosopher" from his cheerful outlook that the universe was

122

founded by chance through a mechanistic combination of atoms; forerunner of Epicurus.

Didymus (c. 309-394): follower of Origen and native of Alexandria.

Diodorus: 4th century A.D. Bishop of Tarsus.

Ebionites: ultra Jewish group of the early Christian church.

Empedocles (c. 490-430 B.C.): Greek philosopher.

Eunapius: Greek sophist in the middle of the fourth century A.D.; supporter of Emperor Julian and opponent of Christianity.

Ennius (239-169 B.C.): called "Father of Roman Poetry."

Ephraim the Syrian (306-373 A.D.): Hymn composer and Biblical commentator.

Eusebius (263?-c. 340): Christian theologian and historian; Bishop of Caesarea; leader of Orthodox group at Council of Nicea.

Gennadius: 5th century A.D. Patriarch of Constantinople.

Gentile: of or pertaining to any people not Jewish; Christian as distinguished from Jewish; heathen or pagan.

Gersonides, Levi ben Gershon (1288-1344): interpreter of Averroism in light of the teachings of Maimonides.

Heraclitus (c. 540-470 B.C.): "The Obscure"; Greek philosopher who believed that change is the basic reality and that wisdom is understanding the hidden harmony of the logos.

Herennius: native of Spain and a senator and quaestor at Rome under Domitian, 1st century.

Hermes Trismegistus: identified with the Greek god Mercury; the Greek name applied to the Egyptian god Thoth, regarded as the source of the "Hermetic" writings on theology and occult subjects; represented by a Latin translation of *Asclepius*, preserved among the works of Apuleius, probably from the first three centuries A.D.

Hermetic: writings of Hermes Trismegistus.

Hermippus of Berita: a Greek grammarian during the 2nd century.

Hermus and Pactolus: small rivers in ancient Lydia; famous for the gold washed from their sand.

Hierotheus: according to Pseudo-Dionysius a religious teacher, otherwise considered a fictitious mystic.

Hipparchus: tutor of Epaminondas, Theban general and statesman in the 4th century B.C.

Homer: great epic poet of Greece, probably c. 9th or 10th centuries B.C.; considered the author of the *Illiad* and the *Odyssey*.

Horace (65-8 B.C.): Roman poet of *Odes, Satires, Epistles,* and *Epodes*, showing a critical view of society from his outlook as a cultured man of his day.

Innocent VIII or Pope Leo X (1475-1521): Italian ecclesiastic and son of Lorenzo de' Medici.

Ionethes or Jonathan the Chaldean: 1st-century translator of sections of the Old Testament into Arabic.

Isaac the Blind: 12th and 13th century Spanish interpreter of the Cabala.

Jamblichus or Iamblichus (c. 250-c. 325 A.D.): Neoplatonist from Syria; probably studied under Porphyry; his *De Mysteriis* is a guide to supernatural study of the time, giving an elaborate exposition of Chaldean theology and a number of commentaries on Plato and Aristotle; much quoted by Proclus.

Jerome, Saint (Eusebius Hieronymus, c. 340-420 A.D.): Christian ascetic and Biblical scholar; chief preparer of the Vulgate version of the Bible.

Josephus, Flavius: 1st century A.D. Jewish historian and general.

Lucan, Marcus A. (39-65 A.D.): Roman poet; born in Spain.

Lysis: Greek scholar of Tarentum in the 4th century B.C.

Manichaen: an adherent of Manichaeism, a Persian philosophy beginning in the 3rd century A.D.

Marinus: a Tuscan; pope from 882-884; bishop of Caere; carried on discussions with Plotius begun under Nicholas.

Medici, Lorenzo de': "Lorenzo the magnificent"; poet and patron of the arts and literature; ruler of Florence (1478-92); father of Leo X.

Melito: bishop of Sardis in Asia Minor in the 2nd century A.D.; Eusebius mentions twenty titles of his writings on philosophical subjects.

Menahem ben Benjamin: Rabbi and Cabalist during the 13th century in Italy, called Manaem.

Moses ben Maimon (1135-1204): "Moses the Egyptian" or "Maimonides"; well known Jewish teacher.

Moses ben Nahman (1195-1270): "Moses of Gerona"; interpreter of the Talmud in Spain.

Neonias: 1st-century A.D. interpreter of the Torah and Jewish law.

Numenius: a 2nd-century Neoplatonist from Syria and a forerunner of Plotinus.

Ophinides, Samuel or Samuel ben Hophni: writer of Arabic commentary on the Pentateuch in the 11th century.

Origen (c. 185-c. 254 A.D.): Alexandrian writer and Christian theologian.

Paul, Saint (c. 5-c. 67): Originally called "Saul of Tarsus"; the apostle to the gentiles; life and doctrines are set forth in the Acts of the Apostles and his Epistles.

Pentateuch: the first five books of the Old Testament; reputed to have been written by Moses.

Peter (? -c. 67): a fisherman on the sea of Galilee; one of the twelve Apostles to Jesus; reputed author of the two New Testament books bearing his name; considered the first pope and founder of the Christian church; also called Simon Peter and Saint Peter.

Plato (427-347 B.C.): Greek philosopher with the belief that physical objects are impermanent representations of unchanging ideas, and that ideas alone give knowledge as they are known by the mind; pupil of Socrates and founder of the Academic School; whose thought had a profound influence upon the development of Christian philosophy.

Philo Judaeus (c. 30 B.C.-c. 40 A.D.): Jewish philosopher, who interpreted the Pentateuch figuratively according to Greek philosophy.

Philolaus: Pythagorean philosopher of the late 5th century B.C.

Plotinus: 3rd century A.D. Roman philosopher; founder of Neoplatonism.

Porphyry (c. 233-c. 304 A.D.): Greek philosopher.

Propertius, Sextus: Roman elegiac poet in the 1st century B.C.

Pseudo-Dionysius (around 4th or 5th century A.D.); author of a number of mystical works; identified during the Middle Ages with Dionysius the Areopagite; although Western theology commonly treated his negative mysticism with reserve, he was more seriously considered by the Eastern Orthodox group.

Pythagoras: Greek philosopher and mathematician of the 6th century B.C.

Remigius: 9th century A.D. Benedictine monk.

Saadia ben Joseph (882-942): Talmudist teacher in Babylonia; known as Sadias.

Saccas, Ammonius: reputed founder of Neoplatonism in the first half of third century A.D.; teacher of Plotinus, as well as Origin of Christian, Longinus, and others.

The Septuagint: the oldest Greek version of the Old Testament, traditionally said to have been translated by 70 or 72 Jewish scholars at the request of Ptolemy II of Egypt in the 3rd century B.C.

Seraphim: plural of Seraph, one of the celestial beings hovering above God's throne in Isaiah's vision. Isaiah, 6.

Severus: 6th century A.D. Bishop of Antioch.

Simeon ben Yohai: author of the Zohar; a Cabalistic writer of the mystical interpretation of the Pentateuch.

Solomon ben Isaac (1040-1105): interpreter of the Bible and the Talmud.

Strabo, Walafrid: German theologian of the 9th century.

Strato (d. c. 270 B.C.): native of Lampsacus and head of the Peripatetic school after Theophrastus.

Talmud: the collection of writings constituting the Jewish civil and religious law; it consists of the Mishnah (text) and the Gemara (commentary), but the term is sometimes restricted to the Gemara.

Theocritus: Greek poet during the 3rd century B.C.

Theodoretus (c. 386-457): Syrian Bishop of Cyrrhus.

Varro, Marcus Terentius; 1st-century B.C. Roman historian and grammarian.

Virgil (70-19 B.C.): his epic the *Aeneid* tells of the origins of the Roman people; his *Eclogue iv*, predicting the birth of a wonder-child to restore the Golden Age was held by some in the Middle Ages to be a prophecy of Christ; representing Reason, acted as Dante's guide in the "Inferno."

126

BIBLIOGRAPHY

The Abington Bible Commentary. Ed. Frederick Carl Eiselen, Edwin
　　Lewis and David G. Downey. New York: Abington Press,
　　1929.
Anton, Charles. *Classical Dictionary*. New York: Harper & Bros.,
　　1852.
Avey, Albert E. *Handbook in the History of Philosophy*, Second Ed.
　　New York: Barnes & Noble, Inc., 1954. (1st printing) 1962
　　(2nd printing).
Biblia Sacra Iuxta Vulgatam Clementinam, Quarta Editio. Ed.
　　Alberto Colunga et Laurentio Turrado. Matriti: Biblioteca De
　　Autores Cristianos, 1965.
Bush, Douglas. *The Renaissance and English Humanism*. Toronto:
　　U. of Toronto Press, 1939.
Cassirer, Ernst, Paul Oskar Kristeller, John Herman Randall, Jr. *The
　　Renaissance Philosophy of Man*. Chicago: The U. of Chicago
　　Press, 1948.
Cruden, Alexander. *A Complete Concordance of the Holy Scriptures
　　of the Old and New Testaments*. Hartford: S.S. Scranton &
　　Co., 1899.
de Santillana, Gingio. *The Age of Adventure*. Boston: Houghton
　　Mifflin & Co., 1957.
Dresden, S. *Humanism in the Renaissance*. New York: McGraw-Hill
　　Book Co., 1968.

Dulles, Avery. *A History of Apologetics*. New York: Westminster Press, 1971.

Giovanni Pico della Mirandola. *De Homininis Dignitate, Heptaplus, De Ente Et Uno*. Ed. Di Eugenio Garin. Florence: Vallecchi Editore, 1942.

Garin, Di Eugenio. *Italian Humanism: Philosophy and Civic Life in the Renaissance*. Trans. Peter Munz. Oxford: Basil Blackwell, 1965.

Greswell, Parr. *Memoirs of Angelus Politianus, Joannes Picus of Mirandula, and Others*. London: Cadall & Davis, 1805.

Greenough, J.B., G. L. Kittredge, G.L. Howard, Benjamin L. D'ooge. *Allen and Greenough's Latin Grammar*. New York: Ginn and Company, 1916.

Hamm, Victor. M. *Pico della Mirandola: Of Being and One*. Milwaukee: Marquette U. Press, 1943.

Hogrefe, Pearl. *The Sir Thomas More Circle*. Urbana: The University of Illinois Press, 1959.

Holy Bible, King James Version. New York: James Pott & Co., 1910.

Hutchinson, Paul and Winfred E. Garrison. *20 Centuries of Christianity*. Harcourt, Brace & Co., 1959.

Hudson, William H. *The Story of the Renaissance*. London: Cassell & Co. Ltd., 1914.

Kristeller, Paul Oskar. *Renaissance Thought. The Classic, Scholastic, and Humanistic Strains*. New York: Harper & Row, 1961.

Lewis, Charlton T. *Latin Dictionary*. New York: Harper & Brothers, 1918.

Morris, William, Ed. *The American Heritage Dictionary of the English Language*. New York: Houghton Mifflin Co., 1969.

Pater, Walter, *The Renaissance*. New York: The New American Library of World Literature, Inc., 1959.

Rogers, Elizabeth Frances. *The Correspondence of Sir Thomas More*. Princeton: Princeton U. Press, 1947.

Runes, Dagobert D. *The Pictorial History of Philosophy*. New York: The Philosophical Library, Inc., 1959.